MASALA & MEATBALLS

INCREDIBLE INDIAN DISHES WITH AN AMERICAN TWIST

Asha Shivakumar

FOUNDER OF FOOD FASHION PARTY

PAGE STREET
PUBLISHING CO.

D1303379

PAGE STREET
PUBLISHING CO.

Copyright © 2017 Asha Shivakumar
Photography copyright © 2017 by Alanna Taylor-Tobin

First published in 2017 by
Page Street Publishing Co.
27 Congress Street, Suite 105
Salem, MA 01970
www.pagestreetpublishing.com

Distributed by Macmillan, sales in Canada by The Canadian Manda Group.

21 20 19 18 17   1 2 3 4 5

ISBN-13: 978-1-62414-388-5

ISBN-10: 1-62414-388-1

Library of Congress Control Number: 2017937022

Cover and book design by Page Street Publishing Co.
Photography by Alanna Taylor-Tobin
Food Styling by Asha Shivakumar

Printed and bound in the United States

As a member of 1% for the Planet, Page Street Publishing protects our planet by donating to nonprofits like The Trustees, which focuses on local land conservation. Learn more at onepercentfortheplanet.org.

To my Mom
and Amma

CONTENTS

INTRODUCTION

As I put the finishing touches on this book, which has been brewing in my mind for years, it's finally turning from a fantasy into a reality.

My visual learning began in a small eight-foot by eight-foot kitchen, observing my amma (grandmum)'s gentle yet deliberate moves as she cooked up meals for her big wonderful family of nine. Her rooftop garden had some of my favorite greens, and in retrospect, I guess my love for green leafy vegetables started there. She would bargain with the fishmonger, leading to a near altercation I was eager to watch. Most days, she cooked three elaborate meals. I loved eating and watching her cook. However, I don't think cooking ever really crossed my mind during those days. My mum, whom I consider a superwoman, could whip up meals for fifty people, just like my amma, in a few hours without breaking a sweat. She taught me how to cook, from the most basic of dishes to the fanciest of meals.

Moving to America after my marriage, miles away from the comfort of my mum's kitchen in India, I had to learn to cook a decent, edible meal. For me, actual cooking came out of necessity. I had an intense need to eat homemade lentils and rice, roti and veggies or a good chicken curry. I couldn't even make a decent coffee to save my life, but I carried a diary full of handwritten recipes from friends and family. I remember the expensive phone calls, the hasty emails that I waited eagerly for my mum to reply to and the innumerable print-outs it would take to cook a simple potato curry. My virtual cooking lessons happened when Skype got popular. I'd ask Mom if that curry looked good, or the dough was too wet. As time passed, I learned, and began to enjoy, cooking. The fancy meals came easily to me; all I had to do was follow a recipe.

My firstborn brought out a whole new world of cooking for me. The little baby bear came along, and I got more creative for his fussy palate. I didn't follow recipes or call as much for directions. I tried to come up with a twist to our normal meals. I began cooking Indian-style fish but putting it in a taco, or chicken strips grilled with Indian spices. I *loved* creating food with a twist. I enjoyed taking American food staples and adding an Indian flair. This book is all about taking comfort food and giving it that curried touch.

In India, the only American foods I knew of were potato burgers, paneer sandwiches and spicy fried chicken. I came to San Francisco, known for its array of different foods. Having an authentic crab chowder with some sourdough absolutely blew my mind. It was similar to a white curry in a way, but so different. When I was introduced to cheese in the form of macaroni and cheese, my mind worked overtime to see how I could add some touch to make it my own. A whole new chicken curry potpie, for example, is one of my favorite delicacies for entertaining.

A dessert that I fell in love with when I was invited for our first Thanksgiving was pumpkin pie. I immediately related it to my favorite pumpkin halwa in Bangalore bakeries. So I just combined the two with my own twist, and pumpkin halwa pie with cardamom was born. Cooking became my love and passion. I felt elated when my family smiled as I brought out my newest creation, thrilled when friends clamored for recipes of party foods, and pumped when they all repeatedly said I needed to write a book.

So I started a blog, Food Fashion Party. I wanted to share my creations, some inspired by my mom and amma, along with many I learned from friends and other blogs. My heart is in my food, and from the beginning, I wanted to share my heart in my blog, and now, in this book. *Masala & Meatballs* is a way of showing my love for food . . . my way of sharing it with you. This is my canvas, and making it vibrant is my purpose. It was almost like my unsaid dreams were becoming a reality, but I would only know months later how much work went into it.

My life has had its ups and downs since the day I started my blog. Perhaps the downs were long, and devastating, but I was able to pull myself back up and pull my life together. Life can throw curveballs at us, but we must persevere. Ultimately, after years, what gave me complete focus was when I got a call to write a book. There it was, a reason for me to wake up with a clear goal. I grabbed this opportunity to turn my life around and take my final step out of the haze.

My approach to this book is simple, and I refuse to call it fusion. It's a book that introduces Indian cooking to those who love the spices but want to have it in a way that's comfortable for them. It's a book for Indian connoisseurs who love a little twist to their traditional food. This book is for beginners, for advanced cooks, for those planning a party, or just for those cooking a romantic meal for two. It's a book that will make your fussy kid lick his plate clean, or your foodie kid enjoy every single bite. This is a book for *you*.

CHAPTER 1

BREAD & BREAKFAST

It's still dark outside. I walk down the stairs to the lull of the morning hours. I grab a handful of granola and sip a bit of coffee before I hear, "What's for breakfast?"

To take you down memory lane . . . there . . . that's me lifting the sheets away, crunching my eyelids looking for Mum and Dad, asking that same question. As usual, I can hear the sound of the pressure cooker, the smell of the cooking dal, the hoots of the boiling milk and the flow of running water. Mum clearly was busy preparing lunch and getting ready to head out to work. She would ask me, "What do you want for breakfast?" Almost always, I would opt for something sweet, something with ghee, and she would whip up a pancake before I could even spell "pancake." She really is something.

I get up early now. Breakfast is quick, but I always try to make it special. I have to say, though, that breakfasts on weekday mornings are usually smoothies or muffins that I made the previous night, or the waffles that I froze a while back. But, come the weekend, a sense of comfort oozes from every bone in my body. I turn on my '80s classics, mix a batch of my mom's pancake recipe and brew coffee. With a generous dollop of melted ghee on the first pancake and my trusty cup of coffee, I stand by the kitchen window, savoring every bite with hope for a beautiful weekend.

So, come along! Here, you'll find the fanciest weekend breakfasts, which will hit the spot every time. Have a breakfast or brunch party. Make tomato grits with fried eggs, or a chive omelet with a peppery bread roll. If you have a craving for carbs, have some yogurt topped with granola, and turn the volume up with saffron and cardamom. When you want to soak in the peace and silence of the morning hours, wake up early, make a beautiful chocolate challah, have some coffee and let the aroma of the baking bread surround you.

Whether you are cooking and baking for company, for the two of you or the sweetest clan, this will make your day very special. As someone said, "Bread and water can so easily be toast and tea."

MUM'S JAGGERY CRÊPES WITH CASHEWS AND COCONUT

Although I was given many options for breakfast during my school and college days, my first choice would be these crêpes. I could eat a huge stack of these. My favorite part was always the dark amber crust that was created by the caramelization of the bigger pieces of jaggery. The coconut and the generous drizzle of ghee on top were just divine.

As I sipped my warm glass of sugary milk (which my little one now calls "Indian milk"), I watched mom dress in a crisp, Bengal cotton sari, ready to leave for work. As I straightened her pleats for her, she reminded me not to forget my lunch box. I smiled as I sent her off to work before I got ready for school.

This crêpe requires very few ingredients, with fresh ghee being the key. Even if you don't cook the crêpe in ghee, just drizzling on a teaspoon when serving will give it a special touch. These are best eaten warm and can be filled with cream and fruits to make them fancier.

SERVES 6–8

2 cups (240 g) all-purpose flour (maida)

⅓ cup (40 g) fine rice flour

¾ cup (90 g) grated jaggery (panela)

⅓ cup (45 g) cashews, broken to small bits

⅓ cup (37 g) freshly grated or thinly sliced coconut

¼ tsp salt

3½ cups (823 ml) water, as needed

Vegetable oil, for frying

Clarified butter or ghee, for serving (optional, but very important for authentic flavor)

In a mixing bowl, combine the flours, jaggery, cashews, coconut and salt. Add ½ cup (120 ml) water at a time and whisk to blend well. The batter should be thin like a crêpe batter. If the batter is too thick, you will not achieve a crispy crêpe.

Heat ½ teaspoon oil in a nonstick pan over medium-high heat, pour a large ladleful of batter into the pan and swirl the pan around to make a thin crêpe. Cook until the sides are brown and crispy, about 1 minute. These are best served hot with a teaspoon of clarified butter melted on top.

SAFFRON MILK BREAD

I once (maybe twice) took a quiz to see what spice I would be, secretly hoping I was saffron. The thought of saffron gives me a warm, fuzzy feeling inside.

Bread making is not all that hard, though I didn't bake bread for the first thirty years of my life. At the time, I only knew good bread and great bread. Living in the sourdough capital, San Francisco, I was inspired to learn more about the art of kneading, the perfect crust, the ideal air pockets. It felt overwhelming to achieve, but once I did, I wondered whether I was a baker's daughter in my last birth.

This is a soft bread that can be used to make wonderful French toast, desserts like fried bread with sweetened milk cream or just toasted with a mug of coffee. Bread dough can be quite fussy with weather. When it's hot and humid, you probably don't require that much water, but in winter you may need a little bit more. Always let the dough rise in a warm place, where it is undisturbed. Fresh yeast is also key to good bread, so if your yeast has been sitting on the shelf for too long, get a new bottle or packet.

MAKES 2 LOAVES

½ cup (120 ml) water, warmed to 110°F (43°C), divided

2¼ tsp (9 g) active dry yeast

½ cup (100 g) plus 2 tsp (8 g) granulated sugar, divided

1½ cups (355 ml) reduced-fat milk

½ cup (112 g) unsalted butter, plus more for brushing loaves

⅓ tsp ground nutmeg

½ tsp lemon zest

¼ tsp saffron

1 tsp salt

5 cups (600 g) all-purpose flour, divided

Oil, for the bowl

CARDAMOM COMPOUND BUTTER

½ cup (112 g) unsalted sweet butter, at room temperature

2 tbsp (16 g) confectioners' sugar

⅓ tsp ground cardamom

In the bowl of a stand mixer (or in a large mixing bowl if mixing by hand), combine ¼ cup (60 ml) water, yeast and 2 teaspoons (8 g) granulated sugar and let it bubble up. The yeast has to be activated for at least 10 minutes. If it does not bubble, discard and use new yeast.

In a saucepan, bring the milk and remaining ¼ cup (60 ml) water to a slow simmer over medium-low heat. Add the butter, remaining ½ cup (100 g) sugar, nutmeg, lemon zest and saffron and let it melt.

After the yeast has bubbled, add the butter-milk-saffron mixture, salt and 4 cups (480 g) flour. Using the dough hook on your stand mixer, start on low speed and let the dough mix and come together. If it is too sticky, add ½ cup (60 g) flour. The dough should not get too dry. Once the dough comes together, turn it out onto a lightly floured surface and knead until smooth, 8 to 10 minutes, or let the machine run on low speed for about 4 minutes.

Lightly oil a mixing bowl, transfer the dough gently to the bowl and brush the top with oil. Cover and let it rise in a warm place for about 1 hour, or until it's doubled in volume.

Prepare 2 small 8 x 4 x 2½-inch (20 x 10 x 6.4-cm) bread loaf tins or 1 large 9 x 5 x 2½-inch (23 x 12.7 x 6.4-cm) tin. Lightly oil and dust the tins with flour and set aside.

Slightly deflate the dough and divide it in half. You can make 3 long strips and braid one part of the dough or make 3 long equal strips and roll them into ropes. Line them beside each other. Take the left rope and bring it next to the middle one, and bring the right rope next to the middle rope. Keep repeating it until you have finished braiding and set them in the pans. Brush them with some butter, cover loosely with a thin towel and let them rise until they are 1 to 2 inches (2.5 to 5 cm) above the pan, 40 to 60 minutes.

Preheat the oven to 350°F (180°C, or gas mark 4).

Bake for 40 to 45 minutes for 2 small pans or about 60 minutes for 1 large pan. If you tap on the bottom and it sounds hollow, then it's done. Remove to a wire cooling rack and let cool completely before slicing.

To make the butter, combine the butter, confectioners' sugar and cardamom in a small bowl. Serve with the bread.

COCONUT CARDAMOM GRANOLA WITH SAFFRON-INFUSED YOGURT

To me, this breakfast can be a dessert, too. It's got everything: the warm spices, the sweetened yogurt and the crunchy granola. You'd be surprised at how simple, and addictive, this can be. Be sure to make an extra sheet pan, just in case. What you add to it is totally up to you. I absolutely love the cranberries, coconut oil and maple syrup combo. For those who live for clusters, you can add a whipped egg white, and not stir it too much while it's baking. Use a lighter-colored baking sheet and line it with parchment paper so the granola doesn't burn.

SERVES 4–6

---

2 cups (160 g) old-fashioned oats

½ cup (55 g) raw sliced almonds

2 tbsp (16 g) sesame seeds

½ tsp salt

¼ cup (60 ml) dark maple syrup, plus more for garnish

¼ cup (60 g) coconut oil

½ tsp ground cardamom

⅓ cup (45 g) whole cashews (optional)

⅓ cup (45 g) halved walnuts (optional)

¼ cup (20 g) grated coconut, toasted (optional)

⅓ cup (40 g) raisins (optional)

⅓ cup (40 g) dried cranberries (optional)

1 cup (245 g) thick yogurt

1 pinch of saffron

2 tsp (10 ml) warm milk

Preheat the oven to 275°F (140°C, or gas mark 1) and line a baking sheet with parchment paper.

Combine the oats, almonds, sesame seeds and salt in a large mixing bowl.

In a small mixing bowl, combine the maple syrup and coconut oil. Microwave for 20 seconds, or melt in a pot over low heat, until warmed. Stir until the coconut oil melts. Pour the mixture over the oats; stir to coat well. Spread a thin layer on the baking sheet and bake for approximately 1 hour, stirring every 10 minutes. In the last 15 minutes of baking, add the cardamom and stir to combine.

Allow to cool for 10 minutes. Add the nuts, coconut and dried fruit, if desired, and stir to combine.

To make the yogurt, crush the saffron, then mix it into the milk. Let it sit for 10 minutes, then swirl it into the yogurt. Top with granola and a drizzle of maple syrup, if desired.

COFFEE-CHOCOLATE WALNUT CHALLAH

A few years ago, on our yearly travel, we decided to visit our dream place, Paris. Our go-to breakfast in Paris was chocolate bread, croissants and thick, creamy hot chocolate. My little baby boy survived with just those three things during those ten beautiful and inspiring days.

One of the many things I missed when I got back was the chocolate bread. I could almost smell and taste it. I tried recreating it, but I could not get the texture or the taste right. Just when I wanted to try my hand for the eighth time, I thought to myself, why try to recreate it? It feels more special left to the imagination, accompanied by nostalgic feelings and memories.

I did come up with my favorite combo—cardamom, coffee and cocoa—during those trials, and it is one of the most loved breads in my home. For coffee addicts, this is a pleasure. A good-quality cocoa powder is a must. As this loaf bakes, get ready to sit by your kitchen, close your eyes and soak in the aroma. It is truly delicious.

MAKES 2 LOAVES

BREAD

2¼ tsp (9 g) active dry yeast or instant yeast

1 tbsp (12 g) granulated sugar

1⅓ cups (315 ml) water, warmed to 110°F (43°C), divided

3 tbsp (42 g) very soft butter (leave at room temperature for 1 hour)

2 large eggs

1 tsp salt

5 cups (600 g) bread flour, plus more as needed

CHOCOLATE CARDAMOM STUFFING

1 cup (135 g) chopped walnuts

2 tbsp (10 g) good-quality cocoa powder (I like Valrhona)

3 tbsp (45 g) brown sugar

⅓ tsp freshly ground cardamom

1 tbsp (8 g) espresso powder or (15 ml) brewed coffee

EGG WASH

1 egg beaten with 2 tbsp (30 ml) water

To make the bread, in a bowl, dissolve the yeast and granulated sugar in ⅓ cup (80 ml) of the warm water and let it bubble up for 5 minutes. This means your yeast is ready to use. If it does not bubble, discard and use new yeast.

In the meantime, in the bowl of a stand mixer (or in a large mixing bowl if mixing by hand) using a dough hook, combine the butter, eggs, salt and bread flour. Slowly add in the yeast mixture and let the machine run on medium speed for 3 minutes. Slowly add about ½ cup (120 ml) of the water to form a dough, adding more water just until you see it come together to form a ball. You might not need all of the water. When all the dough comes together and you see everything is incorporated, turn the machine down to low and let it run for another 6 to 8 minutes. (Alternatively, turn out the dough onto a floured work surface and knead by hand for about 10 minutes.) If the dough seems very sticky, add flour 1 teaspoon at a time until it feels tacky, but no longer sticky. The dough is finished when it is soft and smooth and holds a ball shape.

Transfer the dough to an oiled bowl and let it rise, covered, until doubled in size, or about 45 minutes.

(continued)

COFFEE-CHOCOLATE WALNUT CHALLAH (CONT.)

To make the stuffing, combine the stuffing ingredients in a small bowl. Set aside.

Gently divide the dough into 6 portions. Roll each portion into long rectangle shape, about 13 inches long x 3 inches wide (33 x 7.5 cm). If the dough shrinks as you try to roll them, let them rest for 5 minutes to relax the gluten and then try again. Spread about 2 tablespoons (30 g) of the walnut mixture down the middle of the rectangles. Pinch the sides closed and roll into logs. Repeat for all the dough. Gather the ends of 3 ropes and pinch the top. Take the rope on the left and bring it to the middle, then take the rope on the right and bring it to the middle. Repeat until the ropes are braided and then pinch them together at the bottom. Repeat for the remaining 3 ropes. Transfer the loaves to a baking sheet lined with parchment paper. Cover lightly with a thin towel and let them rise for another 45 minutes.

Preheat the oven to 400°F (200°C, or gas mark 6).

When ready to bake, reduce the temperature to 375°F (190°C, or gas mark 5). Brush the egg wash over the loaves and bake for 35 to 40 minutes, or until golden brown and the bottom sounds hollow when tapped. Transfer to a cooling rack. Slice the bread when it is completely cool.

VEGETABLE SAVORY CAKE

This is inspired by a popular savory cake called handvo from the region of Gujarat. I was just recently introduced to this cuisine, and I am in love.

This is usually eaten as a snack, and I enjoy it during breakfast. I almost always make them in muffin pans to send them off in my boys' lunch boxes with some dip. It's full of vegetables, and tastes as good hot as at room temperature.

SERVES 6–8

1 cup (120 g) coarse semolina flour

½ cup (60 g) chickpea flour

1 cup (240 g) yogurt

¼ cup (60 ml) olive oil

1 tbsp (8 g) baking powder, divided

2 tsp (12 g) salt, divided

1 tbsp (15 ml) fresh lemon juice

1 small carrot

1 small onion

1 red bell pepper

2 tbsp (28 g) ghee

1 tsp cumin seeds

1 tsp mustard seeds

1 tsp asafetida

1" (2.5 cm) piece ginger, grated

3 green chiles, finely chopped

½ cup (70 g) peas

½ cup (40 g) shredded cabbage

½ cup (8 g) cilantro

¼ cup (60 ml) warm water

⅓ cup (43 g) sesame seeds

Preheat the oven to 375°F (190°C, or gas mark 5). Grease a 9-inch (23-cm) springform cake pan, mini tart pans or muffin tins. Alternatively, you can steam this.

In a sauté pan, fry the semolina flour over medium heat for 2 minutes, or until it's a pale golden color. Do not brown it too much. Add the chickpea flour and toast it for 2 minutes, until you smell a nutty aroma. Turn off the heat and transfer the flours to a mixing bowl. Set aside.

In a small mixing bowl, combine the yogurt, olive oil, ½ tablespoon (4 g) of the baking powder, 1½ teaspoons (9 g) of the salt and lemon juice. Mix well and let it sit while you get the vegetables ready.

Peel the carrot and onion and dice them finely. Dice the bell pepper (or use a food processor). Combine the toasted flours and remaining ½ tablespoon (4 g) baking powder in a large bowl. Add the yogurt mixture and blend well.

Warm the ghee in a pan over medium heat. Add the cumin seeds, mustard seeds, asafetida, grated ginger and finely chopped chiles. Sauté for a few minutes, then add the chopped vegetables, peas, cabbage, cilantro and the remaining ½ teaspoon salt and cook just for a couple of minutes; the vegetables should still be crunchy. Turn off the heat and let it cool completely.

Once the veggies are completely cooled, add them to the semolina mixture and blend everything well. The batter should be thick. Check for salt. Add the warm water to the batter and mix thoroughly with a wooden spoon.

(continued)

VEGETABLE SAVORY CAKE (CONT.)

Pour the batter into the prepared pan(s). Sprinkle generously with the sesame seeds. Bake in the center of the oven for 15 minutes, then reduce the temperature to 300°F (150°C, or gas mark 2) and bake for 45 to 60 minutes longer for a large cake or 20 to 25 minutes longer for mini tarts or muffins. Alternatively, you can pour some water into a deep wok, place a stand inside, pour the batter into a 9-inch (23-cm) springform pan, cover and steam for 20 to 25 minutes.

The cake is ready when it is a dark brown color and a toothpick inserted into the center comes out clean. Remove from the oven and cool in the pan for 30 minutes. Take the cake out of the pan, cut into slices and serve warm or cold. This is delicious with a green chutney, pesto or any sauce.

COOKED PANZANELLA SALAD (BREAD UPMA)

This is my take on a panzanella salad. It comes together when there's some crusty bread, a lone carrot and a few sad-looking vegetables that I have to use up. It's the kind of dish I make when it's grocery day, or when I want to just keep it simple, yet comforting, and full of vegetables. I find I make this dish a lot during the summer, probably because it tastes really good packed for a picnic. The bread soaks up anything you put it in, and anything you drizzle over it. You can add any vegetable you like. I particularly like the combination of beans and carrots. The cherry tomatoes just complete the marriage of the flavors. I like my bread soft and juicy when all the flavors soak in. My boys love it lightly crisped up, which still adapts to the vegetable mix. Whether you toast the bread or not, it's incredibly delicious.

SERVES 4

---

1 loaf ciabatta or rustic sourdough bread or 6 Peppery Cumin Buns (page 30), cut into 1" (2.5-cm) cubes (about 6 cups [600 g] bread cubes)

3 tbsp (45 ml) extra virgin olive oil, plus more for drizzling

⅓ tsp pepper

1 tsp cumin seeds

3 shallots, finely sliced lengthwise

3 green chiles, finely sliced

4 cloves garlic, minced

2 carrots, peeled and cut into thin, 2" (5-cm) sticks

½ cup (125 g) beans, thinly sliced lengthwise

⅓ tsp turmeric

10 cherry tomatoes, halved

2 tbsp (30 ml) sweet and spicy sauce or chili sauce

3 tbsp (6 g) roughly chopped basil leaves

1 tsp lemon juice

In a large bowl, combine the bread cubes with a drizzle of oil and the pepper until coated. Toast the bread in a dry pan on the stove top or on a baking sheet in a 300°F (150°C, or gas mark 2) oven for 10 minutes, until slightly crispy on the outside. Do not burn them. Set aside.

Place a large, flat pan over medium heat. Add the 3 tablespoons (45 ml) olive oil and let it get warm, then add the cumin seeds and let them splutter and brown. Add the shallots, green chiles and garlic and sauté until slightly wilted, 1 minute. Add the carrots, beans and turmeric to the pan, decrease the heat to low and cook, covered, for about 5 minutes. You do not need to add water because the vegetables are very thinly cut and they will cook quickly.

Once the vegetables are cooked, add the tomatoes and sauté for a minute. Add the bread cubes to the mixture and toss well to coat with the sauce from the vegetables. Add the chili sauce and basil leaves, drizzle with the lemon juice, toss again and serve warm.

INSTANT NO YEAST NAAN

Making naan at home is as easy as making pizza dough. In fact, it's much easier. I tend to make my naan without yeast most of the time, because it's less time-consuming and tastes just as good. The best thing about making naan at home is that it stays soft for a longer time than store-bought does. Of course, it's also healthier. With naan you can add any toppings, and later turn them into Indian naan pizzas with leftover vegetables.

MAKES 8–10 NAAN

¼ cup (60 g) plain unsweetened yogurt

1 tbsp (8 g) baking powder

1½ cups (355 ml) lukewarm water, divided, plus more as needed

2 cups (240 g) whole wheat flour

2 cups (240 g) all-purpose flour, plus more for rolling

⅓ tsp baking soda

1 tsp salt

½ tsp nigella seeds (optional)

4 cloves garlic, very finely chopped (optional)

1 tbsp (14 g) unsalted butter

In a small bow, combine the yogurt, baking powder and ⅓ cup (80 ml) of the warm water and set aside for a minute or two.

In a large mixing bowl, combine the flours, baking soda and salt. Add the yogurt mixture and the remaining water. Knead to make a semi soft dough. If you need more water, add a little at a time. It should not be very sticky or very hard. Once everything comes together to form a smooth dough, place it in an oiled bowl, cover with a damp towel and let rest for at least 10 minutes.

Knead it for a couple of minutes and let rest for another 2 minutes.

Place a nonstick or a cast-iron pan (which I prefer) over medium-high heat and get it really hot. Take a piece of dough the size of a tennis ball and roll it out on a lightly floured countertop to approximately 10 inches (25 cm). Sprinkle with a few nigella seeds and some garlic, if desired, and roll again so it gets stuck to the dough and doesn't fall off while cooking.

Put the naan on the hot griddle and let it cook for 30 to 40 seconds. When you see a few bubbles on top, turn the naan over and cook the other side, 2 to 3 minutes total. Smear some butter on both sides and serve hot or wrap in a cloth and keep warm until ready to serve.

(continued)

Add flour in the bowl.

Add the yogurt and water and mix with a spoon.

Take the dough out on the counter and knead it.

Let it rest.

Divide into equal portions.

Roll it out to approximately 10 inches (25 cm).

Sprinkle and press the seasame, nigella seeds and garlic.

Once it is cooked on griddle, brush with butter.

APPLE-PISTACHIO WAFFLED FRENCH TOAST

I always think of my dad when I make this French toast, because he had a sweet tooth and made this during the weekends for the three of us. It's truly one of the simplest, yet most compelling breakfasts. Use any bread. Take a chunky piece of good whole-grain bread, dip it in the pistachio mix and let it sizzle in the buttered waffle iron. It creates a crust while keeping the center of the bread soft and sweet. Serve with some confectioners' sugar and fruit. Don't worry if you don't have a waffle iron. A griddle works just as well.

SERVES 4–6

1 red Gala Apple, washed and grated with the skin

3 large eggs

1 cup (235 ml) whole milk

⅓ cup (35 g) ground pistachios

⅓ cup (80 g) packed dark brown sugar

⅓ tsp ground cardamom

Pinch of salt

2 tbsp (28 g) unsalted butter

8–12 slices whole-grain bread

Cream or maple syrup, for serving

In a large mixing bowl, combine the grated apple and eggs and mix well. Add the milk, pistachios, dark brown sugar, cardamom and salt. Mix well and set aside.

Preheat a waffle iron or griddle pan over medium heat and butter it.

Liberally dip each slice of bread in the egg-milk mixture and place it on the waffle iron or griddle. Cook until brown on one side, then flip and brown the other side. Place on a cooling rack and repeat with the remaining bread, adding more butter to the waffle iron or griddle as necessary. Serve with some cream or a drizzle of maple syrup.

PEPPERY CUMIN BUNS

"The smell of good bread baking, like the sound of lightly flowing water, is indescribable in its evocation of innocence and delight," M. F. K. Fisher wrote. I couldn't agree more. Walking into a bakery creates a sensory overload, especially when I've had a long day. Mom would come home in the evening, passing the Iyengar Bakery (a famous bakery in the southern part of India), and she would often buy the masala buns. This is a recipe created for her, and an ode to her love of spicy bread. You can add any spices you like, but just be sure to keep the measurements the same, and you will get a good, soft roll every time. I like to stuff it with vegetables, toast it with some compound butter and enjoy it with a cup of strong coffee.

MAKES 6

⅔ cup (160 ml) water, warmed to 110°F (43°C)

1 tsp active dry yeast

1 tsp granulated sugar

2⅓ cups (280 g) all-purpose flour

1 tsp salt

2 tbsp (28 g) unsalted butter, melted, plus more for brushing

½ tsp cumin seeds

½ tsp coarsely crushed black pepper

1 tsp nigella seeds, for garnish

6 cilantro leaves, for garnish

In the bowl of a stand mixer (or in a large bowl if mixing by hand), combine the warm water, yeast and sugar and let it stand for 10 minutes. If it does not bubble, discard and use new yeast.

Add the all-purpose flour, salt, butter, cumin and black pepper to the yeast mixture. Using a dough hook on the stand mixer, let the mixer run on low speed first. Once the dough comes together, turn the mixer on high and let it run for 5 minutes. The dough will start to be a little sticky, but do not add more flour. Keep mixing and bringing everything together. Turn it out onto a lightly floured surface and knead for 5 minutes. Then put the dough in an oiled bowl, cover and keep in a warm place for 2 hours to rise.

After 2 hours, lightly punch down the dough, divide into 6 equal portions and form into any shape you want. Place the rolls on a sheet pan 2 inches (5 cm) apart. Let rise again for at least an hour, or until doubled in size.

Preheat the oven to 400°F (200°C, or gas mark 6).

Brush the tops of the rolls with butter, milk or egg wash and sprinkle with some nigella seeds or decorate with a cilantro leaf. Bake for about 20 minutes, or when you tap the bottom of the bun it sounds hollow. Remove from the oven and brush lightly with butter. Serve warm with coffee or make into a sandwich.

FRIED BANANA BREAD (AKA MANGALORE BUNS)

While one side of the globe was frying bread and calling it fried bread, we called it Mangalore buns (banana puri). This comes from Mangalore, a land of pretty ladies, they say.

I feel extremely lucky to have friends like family in every stage of my life. Moving from a cozy apartment to our own home was a new venture, and an exciting one. My very pretty neighbor and I formed a bond over the fence. From passing a cup of sugar or liquid detergent, nothing was out of bounds when it came to needing something urgent. One rainy day she shared this banana puri with spicy lentil curry. All I could say was that I wanted more. Served with something spicy, it makes the slight sweetness of the puri a bit subtler and the sharp spice of the curry a bit milder. It's a little deviation from the usual puri (a deep-fried flatbread); this has a bit of a spongier and denser feel to it, with a breadlike texture.

SERVES 14–16

2 ripe bananas

2 tbsp (28 g) thick full-fat non-sour yogurt

⅓ tsp baking soda

1 tsp baking powder

1 tsp salt

2½ cups (300 g) all-purpose flour, plus more as needed

Vegetable oil, for deep-frying

1 tbsp (8 g) nigella seeds

Add the bananas to a mixing bowl and mash well. Add the yogurt, baking soda, baking powder and salt and mix well. Add the flour and mix it slowly with a wooden spatula until everything comes together. Flour your clean hands lightly, turn it out onto a floured surface and knead the dough slowly. If the dough is wet, add more flour, 1 tablespoon (8 g) at a time, and roll it back and forth to get it smooth. Place the dough in a bowl, cover and let rest for 2 hours.

Pour the vegetable oil into a pot to a depth of 3 to 4 inches (7.5 to 10 cm), place over medium-high heat and bring to 350°F (180°C) on a deep-frying thermometer.

Divide the dough into 14 to 16 equal portions. Add some nigella seeds to each piece and roll them to about 4 inches (10 cm) in diameter and ½ inch (1.3 cm) thick. Carefully add the rolls to the hot oil in batches and fry them over medium to medium-low heat for about a minute on each side, or until golden brown. Remove from the oil with a spider and drain on paper towels. Bring the oil back up to temperature in between batches.

MUSHROOM AND CHIVE OMELET

Chaat masala in eggs has become a must at our home. The "king egg," created by my little one, contains everything but the kitchen sink. He says, "Chaat masala is my secret ingredient." So now, when I make omelets with chaat masala, he definitely takes all the credit.

I've used green chilies and red chili powder, both of which I think lend a different kind of heat to eggs, and milk just makes it fluffier. This is the classic egg omelet I grew up with, sans the mushrooms and chives. Make it on the stove top or bake it in the oven; both work well. It's a perfect weekend breakfast.

SERVES 4

1 tbsp (15 ml) olive oil

½ red onion, chopped

2 green chiles, finely chopped

½ cup (35 g) cleaned and finely chopped shitake mushrooms (about 15 mushrooms)

4 large eggs

2 tbsp (30 ml) full-fat cream or milk

⅓ tsp chaat masala

⅓ tsp red chili powder

⅓ tsp turmeric

2 tbsp (2 g) finely chopped chives

½ tsp salt

½ tsp freshly ground black pepper

Toasted bread with butter, for serving

Add the olive oil to a medium-sized sauté pan or cast-iron pan over medium heat and let it get hot. Add the red onion and sauté for 30 seconds. Add the green chiles and mushrooms and sauté until the mushrooms are fully cooked, about 2 minutes.

Meanwhile, in a mixing bowl, combine the eggs, cream, chaat masala, chili powder, turmeric, chives, salt and pepper. Whisk it well until it is frothy and light. Add the egg mixture to the pan and turn the heat to low. You can continue to cook on the stove top, covered, or transfer to a 350°F (180°C, or gas mark 4) oven for 20 minutes.

Serve hot with some toasted buttered bread.

CHAPTER 2

STARTERS, SNACKS & SIDES

They were the size of tennis balls. They took one, and enjoyed it and looked content for the next few hours. Bonda, a potato-stuffed chickpea-coated deep-fried fritter, was the appetizer that day. Little did I know at the time that it was a gut-bulging snack. It was so good, nevertheless. That day, dinner was delayed and we had leftovers.

My experiences in the kitchen started with snacks. My mum says this even today: "Don't fill your tummy with snacks." While I love making elaborate meals, there's something very comforting about deep-fried bites and quick snacks with cups of coffee and long conversations.

Indians consider their tea and coffee time ritual very sacred. Then, it was a knock on the door and "What are you making?" that started a conversation that dragged on for a couple of hours. There were coffee and tea cups on the table, empty plates of fried spinach fritters and some homemade cookies. Two hours later, you see a surprised emoji look on the neighbor's face. "Oh, I have to go make dinner, the husband will be home soon."

Now, there's a call. Stop by, let's chat over coffee, it's been a while. The coffee pot is hot, the oil is almost at the smoking point and the doorbell rings. There goes the first sizzle, the first batch of onion is dipped into chickpea batter and is frying, soon to be set on a plate with multiple chutneys and dips.

This chapter could take up the whole book, but I had to restrain myself. You'll find some of my favorites in it. On some days, I just make chutney sandwiches or a huge platter of Masala Chicken Wings (page 62) and we call it a night. My boys love when I make Spiced Popcorn (page 39) and crispy baked chickpeas. They pile it into paper cones and impress their friends. Make a lamb patty (page 59), top it with some sauce, and it is perfect on a cold day with some tea. That same patty works amazingly stuffed in a burger or as a side with some quick fried rice.

This chapter is all about multitasking recipes to incorporate them into other meals. It's about taking simple things and amping them up a tiny bit to entertain your guests. Because even if they're "snacks," every bite should be an experience.

SPICED POPCORN THREE WAYS

There are countless variations for making popcorn. Pop the corn, add any spice combination and it becomes your own creation. One of our favorite Indian snacks is chivda, a combination of puffed rice, peanuts and spices. I've made a variation of that with popcorn, and I think it is one of my favorite flavors—sweet and spicy.

Chaat masala is another spice combination that contains black salt, mango powder, pepper and many other ingredients. Add that to melted butter, toss it with popcorn and your kids will think you're a genius. It doesn't take a lot to impress the adults, but kids—that's another ballgame. This is tried and tested with kids, so go ahead and impress them!

MAKES 8 CUPS (400 G)

3 tbsp (45 ml) coconut, peanut or canola oil

⅓ cup (65 g) high-quality popcorn kernels

1 tbsp (14 g) unsalted butter, or as needed (optional)

Salt to taste

SWEET AND SPICY PEANUT CHILI

1 tbsp (15 ml) vegetable oil

1 tsp chili powder

½ cup (73 g) toasted salted peanuts

1 tbsp (14 g) brown sugar

CHAAT MASALA

1 tbsp (15 ml) coconut, peanut or canola oil

⅓ tsp turmeric

GARLIC MINT PEPPER

2 tbsp (30 ml) olive oil

3 cloves garlic, crushed or pounded

10 whole mint leaves

½ tsp freshly ground black pepper

Heat the oil in a 3-quart (2.7-L) heavy-bottomed saucepan over medium-high heat. If you are using coconut oil, allow all of the solid oil to melt.

Put 3 or 4 popcorn kernels into the oil. When the kernels pop, add the remaining popcorn kernels in an even layer. Cover the pan, remove from the heat and wait 1 minute. Return the pan to the heat. The popcorn will pop. Once you hear the popping, shake the pan carefully, cracking the lid 1 inch (2.5 cm) to release the steam. Once you hear the popping stop, remove from the heat and pour into a large bowl. Drizzle with butter and sprinkle with salt, or add one of the desired flavorings.

To make one of the flavorings, in a separate pan, combine the oil and seasonings over medium heat. Cook the spices for a minute and then drizzle the mixture evenly over the popcorn and toss to combine.

HUSH PUPPIES (RICE BONDAS) WITH PEPPER AND CUMIN

The first time I had hush puppies was at the Boxing Room, a Cajun restaurant in San Francisco. I couldn't stop eating them. It soon dawned on me that they are very similar to bonda, a popular snack in South India. Indians definitely love their fried food. Monsoon season arrives, and the ladies start deep-frying everything. There are many versions of bonda with different grains. Here, I've shown you one very popular Mangalore version that my grandma used to make with some green leafy vegetables that she grew in her small garden. This is a classic Southern dish combined with a classic Indian dish. These are slightly denser than the traditional hush puppies, and darker because we use rice flour.

SERVES 4–6

½ cup (60 g) white rice flour

½ cup (60 g) all-purpose flour

1 cup (150 g) plain cornmeal (not the mix)

1 tsp sugar

½ tsp baking powder

¼ tsp baking soda

1 tsp cumin seeds

½ tsp freshly ground black pepper (optional)

Pinch of asafetida (optional)

½ tsp salt

1 cup (40 g) packed amaranth leaves, washed, patted dry and finely chopped

½ cup (120 ml) buttermilk, soured on the countertop for a few hours

½ red onion, finely chopped

2 green chiles, finely chopped, or to taste (seeds removed for less heat, if desired)

Vegetable oil, for deep-frying

In a medium-sized bowl, whisk together the flours, cornmeal, sugar, baking powder, baking soda, cumin seeds, black pepper, asafetida and salt. Add the chopped amaranth leaves and whisk to combine.

Pour the buttermilk into the flour mixture and stir together until smooth but some lumps remain. The batter should be the consistency of a thick pancake batter. Fold in the onion and green chiles. Let the batter rest for 20 minutes on the countertop.

Heat the oil in a Dutch oven or in a *kadai* (a round-bottomed pan for deep-frying) over high heat to 350°F (180°C) on a deep-frying thermometer, adjusting the heat to maintain the temperature. Line a rimmed baking sheet with paper towels.

Using a mini ice-cream scoop or with the help of 2 teaspoons, drop the batter very carefully into the hot oil. Don't crowd the pan too much. Fry 5 to 8 at a time. Fry for 2 minutes and then turn the hush puppies until deep golden brown, about 2 minutes longer. Remove the hush puppies from the oil with a skimmer. Transfer to the prepared baking sheet. Repeat with the remaining batter. Serve warm.

CRACKER CHAAT

Indian chaat is probably one of the most popular food categories that both Indians and non-Indians enjoy. Chaat is just a name for a variety of dishes that have a few core similarities. It's street food, sold in small carts and shops. I remember when my cousin and I would walk for thirty minutes just to have a kachori, a circular deep-fried dough stuffed with different sauces and topped with sev (a fried chickpea noodle). We would eat two, pack two and walk back happily just to eat a huge dinner.

Chaat has many small parts that have to be prepared ahead, and it can be time-consuming. So, it is definitely a treat and not an everyday ordeal. But when you want to eat chaat and not go through the trouble of frying up puris (crunchy, hollow, fried bread) or making sweet chutney, this is an absolutely fantastic alternative. I make cracker chaat almost every time someone comes home. It has very few ingredients, and it gives the feeling, taste and look of chaat. I've tried this with many kinds of crackers, and the best kind are the butter crackers. These are something you want to make after the guests arrive, while they are ready for appetizers. The downside to this is it can get soggy as it sits, but that's never been a problem for me. Trust me, they will be gone before you realize it.

SERVE 2–4

---

1 red onion

1 tomato

½ cup (120 g) thick Greek yogurt

1 tsp sugar

½ tsp toasted cumin seeds, ground

⅓ tsp salt

16 butter crackers (I like Cabaret crackers)

1 recipe Apple Cilantro Chutney (page 162)

6 sprigs cilantro, finely chopped

⅓ cup (50 g) fried chickpea noodles (sev)

Finely dice the onion and set aside. Cut the tomato in half, remove the seeds and pulp and finely dice the flesh.

In a small bowl, combine the yogurt, sugar, cumin and salt. Pour into a sauce bottle with a tiny nozzle.

Arrange the crackers on a plate, drizzle with a teaspoon of the yogurt sauce, sprinkle with the onion and tomato and top with ⅓ teaspoon of the chutney. Sprinkle with some cilantro and the chickpea noodles and serve immediately.

SPICED BALSAMIC COCKTAIL NUTS

These spiced nuts are quick, easy and perfect for gifting. When you have kids, you know you have to get creative with gifting teachers. I absolutely love making them in huge batches and just keeping them handy. These are a perfect combination of heat and spice from the curry powder and a mild, sweet tang from the balsamic vinegar. I find that the balsamic vinegar gives it a darker look and really elevates the flavor of the spiced nuts.

MAKES 3 CUPS (410 G)

1 cup (145 g) raw unsalted cashews

1 cup (120 g) raw unsalted walnuts

1 cup (145 g) raw unsalted almonds

2 cloves garlic, finely grated

½ tsp curry powder

½ tsp cayenne pepper

Sea salt, to taste

Pinch of dried herbs, such as thyme, rosemary or dill (optional)

2 tbsp (30 ml) balsamic vinegar

2 tbsp (30 ml) vegetable oil or melted unsalted butter

2–3 tbsp (30–45 g) brown sugar

Preheat the oven to 325°F (170°C, or gas mark 3). Line a baking sheet with parchment paper.

In a large bowl, combine the nuts, garlic, curry, cayenne, salt and dried herbs, if using. In a separate small bowl, combine the balsamic vinegar, oil and brown sugar. Pour over the nuts and toss to coat. Spread onto the prepared baking sheet and bake on the middle rack for 15 to 20 minutes, tossing every few minutes. Do not let it burn or darken too much.

Remove from the oven and let cool very well before transferring to jars. These make great gifts.

ONION RINGS WITH WASABI AIOLI

One day my mind was set on some good onion rings. The onion rings were ready to be deep-fried when I realized I had no vegetable oil. So I took out a bag of potato chips, crushed them, used them to coat the onions and then baked them. We loved it!

The key to a crispy, baked onion ring is not to crowd them and to bake them on a rack atop a baking sheet. Bake two trays at a time.

SERVES 4

1 cup (120 g) all-purpose flour, divided

1 tsp salt, divided

½ tsp freshly ground black pepper

½ tsp garam masala, divided

½ tsp chili powder (optional)

¼–½ cup (60–120 ml) water

2 (8-oz [227-g]) bags your favorite potato chips (I used Indian-style Lays)

2 large onions, cut horizontally into rings, separated and dried on a paper towel to remove moisture

Cooking oil spray or 2 tbsp (30 ml) vegetable oil

WASABI AIOLI

¼ cup (60 g) low-fat mayonnaise

1 clove garlic, finely minced

¼ tsp wasabi powder

¼ tsp lemon juice

Preheat the oven to 325°F (170°C, or gas mark 3). Line a baking sheet with parchment paper and place a rack on top.

Place 3 shallow bowls on your countertop. In one bowl, combine ½ cup (60 g) of the flour with ½ teaspoon of the salt, pepper and ¼ teaspoon of the garam masala. In another bowl, combine the remaining ½ cup (60 g) flour, remaining ½ teaspoon salt, remaining ¼ teaspoon garam masala and the chili powder. Add the water, starting with ¼ cup (60 ml) and adding more as needed, and stir to make a pancake batter consistency.

Grind the chips into a coarse powder in a food processor and add to the last bowl.

Lightly dredge an onion ring into the plain flour mixture, then dip it into the batter, shake off the extra and finally dip it into the chips mixture. Place on the rack. Repeat with all the onion rings. Spray or brush the onion rings with a little oil. Bake for 20 to 30 minutes, turning every 10 minutes so the onions don't brown too much. Meanwhile, mix all the ingredients for the aioli in a small bowl. Serve the onion rings with the Wasabi Aioli.

CHICKPEA-ROASTED GARLIC FRIES

When there was no vegetarian side for our rice and dal, my cousins and I would make a quick chickpea pancake with some onions, spices and cilantro. Indians use a serious amount of chickpeas in their cooking. You know, I would go to the extent of saying that regular Indian food is largely vegan and gluten-free. I changed the recipe a bit to make these chickpea polenta fries, which are not only gluten-free but also easy to make.

Here, the roasted garlic adds a lot sweetness without overpowering the dish. The Pecorino is a great addition too, but you can use feta cheese instead, or even crumbled, soft paneer. The cooking of the chickpea batter is the only part you'll use your muscles for. After that, it goes in the refrigerator, and then you panfry them. I panfry them only when ready to serve, so that they're fresh and warm. Top it on your green salad and you have a hearty meal.

SERVES 4

1 cup (240 g) Greek-style yogurt

1½ cups (355 ml) water

1 cup (120 g) chickpea flour

1 tbsp (12 g) sugar

1 tsp turmeric

1 tsp black pepper

2 tsp salt

⅓ cup (35 g) grated Pecorino Romano

1 head roasted garlic, cloves squeezed and mashed

½ cup (8 g) cilantro, finely chopped

1 tsp cumin seeds, toasted and ground

1 tsp mango powder

⅓ cup (80 ml) vegetable oil

1 recipe Almond Curry Sauce (page 163)

In a medium-sized bowl, combine the yogurt, water, chickpea flour, sugar, turmeric, black pepper and salt. Whisk the mixture to make a smooth batter without any lumps. Check for seasoning.

Add the yogurt-chickpea mixture to a large, heavy-bottomed nonstick pan and cook over medium heat, stirring continuously, for 30 to 40 minutes, until the mixture becomes thick and has the consistency of soft dough. Quickly add the Pecorino, mashed roasted garlic, cilantro, toasted ground cumin and mango powder. Mix well. Remove from the heat and transfer to an 8-inch (20-cm) greased baking pan, smoothing the top with a rubber spatula. Put the pan in the fridge for 30 minutes to set well.

Once the chickpea mixture is set, cut it into desired-sized squares. Heat the oil in a skillet, add the chickpea squares in batches and sear over medium heat until the crust is crispy on all sides. Serve with the sauce.

CORN-ONION-CASHEW FRITTERS

Have I mentioned before that Indians have an intense relationship with their fried snacks and tea/coffee time? They do. They fry up everything, and I am no exception. There are many kinds of pakoras (fritters), such as the popular potato bajji, onion fritter and vegetable pakora.

I enjoy this combination of corn and cashews. When you find fresh corn, it's the best. The sweet corn and the crunch from the cashews create such a nice mix. A perfect pakora has enough batter to coat the corn, onion and cashews without drowning them. You should still be able to see the shape of the cashews and the corn peeking through after it's fried. The batter has to be thick and almost crumb-like to get the best crispy bite.

SERVES 4

1 cup (150 g) fresh corn off the cob

½ red onion, chopped

½ cup (70 g) whole cashews

1 tsp chili powder

1 tsp salt

⅓ tsp turmeric

½ tsp cumin seeds

1 tbsp (15 ml) vegetable oil

1 cup (120 g) chickpea flour

¼ cup (60 ml) water, or as needed

Any flavorless oil, for deep-frying (I use vegetable oil)

In a mixing bowl, combine the corn, onion, whole cashews, chili powder, salt, turmeric, cumin seeds and vegetable oil and mix everything very well. Let it sit for 15 minutes.

After 15 minutes, add the chickpea flour and, using your clean hands, massage and mix everything together. Add the water, 1 tablespoon (15 ml) at a time, to bring everything together. You will have a sticky dough. When you drop it into the hot oil, it should hold its shape.

Pour the oil into a large, deep pot or a deep fryer to a depth of 3 to 4 inches (7.5 to 10 cm) and bring to 375°F (190°C) on a deep-frying thermometer.

Drop 1 tablespoon (15 ml) of the batter into the oil and fry on one side for a couple of minutes, and then turn it very carefully with a slotted spatula to cook and brown on the other side for another 2 minutes. Remove from the oil with a spider and drain on a paper towel. Repeat with the remaining batter, bringing the oil back up to temperature between batches. Serve hot.

GRILLED CORN ON THE COB WITH LIME CHILI SAUCE

On the corner of the street, this man stands with his blue wooden cart. To one side of his cart, on a small wooden stand, sits a shallow iron wok filled with charcoal. It's red, blazing and ready to crackle up some corn. We walk up to him and choose the best corn. He pulls back the husk, holds it by the handle and keeps turning and cooking the corn over the open flame. I soak in the crackling sound of the corn and the tiny sparks that the charcoal emits as he fans it. After about four minutes, it looks done, and he asks if we need the spicy chutney. Mum and I nod. Our enthusiasm means he goes all out. He takes a lemon wedge, dips it into salty chili powder and rubs it vigorously over the corn. Then he takes it again to the coals to seal in the flavors. He takes a few extra husks, carefully nestles the corn in them and hands it over to us for a few rupees each. Man, that first bite—the strings that get caught in between our teeth and the eyes watering from the spice. It's all the pleasure of simple food. The food that doesn't take much to satiate us. It's the food of our soul.

This is a simple, chili butter corn that we enjoy just as much as I enjoyed the corn on the streets. We now make it on our charcoal grill. It's the life of our summer parties.

SERVES 4

---

4 fresh corn on the cob

2 tbsp (28 g) unsalted butter, softened

1 tsp green chile paste (from about 3 green chiles)

1 tbsp (15 ml) lime juice

⅓ tsp salt

Heat an outdoor grill, preferably a charcoal one. Pull the husk off the corn and tie it together in the back.

In a small bowl, mix together the butter, green chile paste, lime juice and salt.

Put the corn on the hot grill and grill until it is almost cooked and charred, about 4 minutes. Brush the spiced butter on the corn and grill it for another minute or two, or until it is fully cooked.

CHUTNEY SANDWICHES WITH WHIPPED GOAT CHEESE SPREAD

"Want some tea with your sandwiches?" (Said in a European accent). Chutney sandwiches always remind me of the English tea parties I had with my pretend friends, with my pretentious accent and real sandwiches (which I ate).

Bombay sandwiches, smothered in butter or chutney, are very popular. I love this version with the whipped rich goat cheese and the cilantro chutney combo. This is just a base. You can add any spice to the cheese mixture to make it your own. Add a few slices of cooked potato, or maybe even some mashed beans to make it a light lunch.

SERVES 4

3 oz (84 g) goat cheese

2 oz (56 g) cream cheese spread

Pinch of cayenne pepper

⅓ tsp toasted ground cumin

1 tbsp (15 ml) cream or full-fat milk

8 slices rye or dense multigrain bread

1 recipe Apple Cilantro Chutney (page 162)

1 cucumber, thinly sliced

Handful of alfalfa sprouts

Olive oil, for drizzling

Sea salt and freshly ground black pepper

In a food processor, combine the goat cheese, cream cheese, cayenne pepper, ground cumin and cream and process until well blended. Scrape the mixture into a bowl and keep chilled until you are ready to use it.

Cut the bread into any shape you want, or leave as is. Spread the goat cheese mixture on 4 slices of bread and the chutney on the other 4 slices. Place a few cucumber slices and a generous bunch of alfalfa sprouts on top of the chutney. Drizzle with a little oil, sprinkle with some sea salt and a twist of pepper and top the bread slices with the goat cheese mixture facing down. Press together and serve at room temperature.

SPRING ROLLS WITH SPICED POTATOES AND LEEKS

When I was a finance student, constantly looking at numbers and thinking made me hungry. Late-night eating was normal. Cooking at night was not an option. So, a bag of chips or leftovers was all I reached for. The few weekends that I prepared ahead, I would make a huge batch of samosas or spring rolls with leftover dry masalas, and freeze all of it. As you should know by now, I still loved my deep-fried food. So all I had to do was take the batch out, defrost it and deep-fry everything at 11:00 p.m., waking up the hubby to join me in my binges. It brings back memories of those peaceful nights, when all I cared about was getting through my exams and, yes, what food to take to school the next day to impress my friends.

This version of spring rolls is so good with the leeks. The bell peppers are a nice, crunchy addition. Fry them over medium heat so the spring roll wrappers cook through. Make a huge batch, line them up on a baking sheet, freeze them and bag them for when you are ready to deep-fry. Make sure you let them come to room temperature before frying, so they cook through and the temperature of the oil does not drop.

MAKES 20–24 SPRING ROLLS

---

5 red, russet or white potatoes

2 leek stalks

1 bell pepper

2 tsp (10 ml) vegetable oil

1 tsp cumin seeds

Pinch of asafetida

½ tsp red chili powder or 2 green chiles, grated, or ½ tsp chile paste

⅓ tsp turmeric

⅓ tsp chaat masala

½–1 tsp salt

20–24 spring roll wrappers

Beaten egg white or 2 tsp (6 g) cornstarch mixed with 2 tbsp (30 ml) water

Vegetable or canola oil, for deep-frying

Ketchup, for serving

Hot sauce, for serving

Place the potatoes in a large pan, cover with cold water and bring to a boil over high heat. Lower the heat, cover and cook for about 15 minutes, or until the potatoes are fork tender. Do not overcook them. Drain the water and let cool, uncovered. Peel and mash the potatoes and set aside.

Slice the leeks thinly and put them into a large bowl of water. Separate the rings and wash very well so the dirt settles to the bottom. Remove the leeks with a spider ladle, letting the dirt remain undisturbed on the bottom, and dry completely on a dish towel or a paper towel. Core, seed and finely chop the bell pepper. Set aside.

In a large, flat-bottomed pan, heat the oil over medium heat, add the cumin seeds and asafetida and fry for a minute, or until it splutters. Add the leeks, bell pepper, red chili powder, turmeric, chaat masala and salt and sauté for a couple of minutes. Once it is cooked a bit, but still has a bite to it, add the mashed potatoes and mix well to combine. Let cook and dry for a minute or two and then remove from the heat. Let cool completely.

Now take one wrapper and add 2 heaping tablespoons (30 g) of mix and roll into a spring roll. Seal the edges with egg white or cornstarch and water mix. Make all the spring rolls and set aside.

Pour the oil into a pot to a depth of 3 to 4 inches (7.5 to 10 cm) and bring to 375°F (190°C) on a deep-frying thermometer. Slowly add the spring rolls, 3 at a time; do not crowd the pan. Let them brown slowly and cook through, which will take 2 to 3 minutes. Remove with a slotted spoon and drain on paper towels.

Serve with ketchup mixed with your favorite hot sauce.

BRUSCHETTA WITH SPICED EGGPLANT (EGGPLANT BHURTHA)

Call me crazy, but I am allergic to eggplant and still eat it. I hated the vegetable with all my heart while growing up, but I passionately love it now. Why do we love something so much when it hurts?

The name of this dish does not do it justice. You have to make it, put it together, and it will still not speak to you. Until you take a bite. All the layers will sing to you, loudly and deliciously. Try not to skip toasting the bread, and definitely add the fresh onions and tomatoes, as well as the chutney, another key ingredient.

SERVES 4–6

1 large eggplant

2 tbsp (30 ml) canola oil, divided

10 cloves garlic, crushed, divided

½″ (1.3-cm) piece fresh ginger, peeled and grated

1 small red onion, finely diced, plus more for serving

2 green chiles, finely chopped

1 large ripe tomato, finely chopped, plus more for serving

½ tsp salt

⅓ tsp turmeric

½ tsp Kashmiri red chili powder

½ cup (75 g) frozen peas

⅓ tsp garam masala

1 baguette

Olive oil, for brushing and drizzling

½ cup (75 g) crumbled paneer

1 recipe Apple Cilantro Chutney (page 162)

Chopped cilantro or basil, for garnish

Preheat the oven to 450°F (230°C, or gas mark 8) for 15 minutes.

Wash the eggplant well and dry it. Brush some canola oil all over the eggplant, make 5 to 6 slits around it and stuff with 4 of the garlic cloves. Place on a baking sheet and bake for 30 to 40 minutes, or until fork tender. Remove from the oven, let cool and then carefully peel the skin away and mash it with a fork.

Meanwhile, place a large sauté pan over medium heat. Add the remaining canola oil, the remaining 6 crushed garlic cloves and the ginger and sauté for 30 seconds. Add the red onion and green chiles and sauté for a minute or two, until softened. Add the tomato, salt, turmeric and Kashmiri red chili powder, stir to combine and continue to cook until the tomatoes disintegrate and come together into a sauce, 10 minutes. Add the peas, mashed eggplant and garam masala, lower the heat and keep stirring and cooking for another 5 minutes, until you see the oil ooze from the sauce. Turn off the heat and set aside.

Slice the baguette into ⅓-inch (8-mm) slices on a diagonal, brush with some olive oil and toast until golden. Top each slice with the eggplant mixture, crumbled paneer, chopped onion and tomato and chutney, and then drizzle it with some olive oil. Sprinkle with cilantro and serve immediately.

CURRIED PEANUT DIP WITH NAAN CHIPS

This dip, for some reason, has become a regular at home. The boys smother it on sandwiches, spread it on rotis and even mix it with rice. This is a take on a vegetable chutney, with toasted peanuts and a fun, salty twist with the feta. When you dip a chip, be sure to scoop all the layers for the perfect experience. You can use natural peanut butter too, but I find plain old toasted peanuts add that extra fresh crunch to the dip. Serve it with any chips. I find that the simplest work the best.

SERVES 4–6

NAAN CHIPS

4 large naan

1 tbsp (15 ml) olive oil

½ tsp chili powder

Salt and pepper

DIP

1 tbsp (15 ml) vegetable oil

1 large shallot, chopped

1 tbsp (10 g) minced fresh garlic

1 tsp curry powder

⅛ tsp red pepper flakes

2 large carrots, finely chopped

Salt and freshly ground pepper

½ cup (70 g) toasted unsalted peanuts

4 tsp (20 ml) fresh lime juice

1 tbsp (15 ml) soy sauce

1 tsp packed brown sugar

1 tbsp (10 g) crushed salted peanuts

1 tbsp (1 g) finely chopped cilantro

1 tbsp (8 g) crumbled feta cheese

To make the naan chips, preheat the oven to 400°F (200°C, or gas mark 6) for 15 minutes.

Cut the naan into quarters and place them on a baking sheet. Brush them with the olive oil and sprinkle the chili powder and salt and pepper to taste. Toast them in the oven for 10 to 15 minutes, or until completely crispy. Let them cool completely before serving with the dip.

To make the dip, heat the oil in a nonstick skillet over medium heat. Add the shallot and garlic; sauté until the shallot is tender, about 3 minutes. Add the curry powder and red pepper flakes. Stir until aromatic, about 15 seconds. Add the carrots, season with salt and pepper to taste and sauté until the carrots are soft and cooked halfway. Stir in the toasted peanuts, lime juice, soy sauce and brown sugar; toss and sauté until everything is mixed well and incorporated. Turn off the heat. Season with salt and pepper. Let cool completely.

Transfer to a food processor and grind to a coarse paste. Scrape into a bowl and garnish with the crushed salted peanuts, chopped cilantro and feta cheese. Serve with the naan chips.

SPINACH FRITTERS (PAKORAS)

One thing that interested me the most about my amma was her mini rooftop garden. Amma had a green thumb. She grew herbs and green leafy vegetables in little pots and sent me to pick the greens for pakoras, our evening snack. Those were probably the freshest, tastiest and most organic greens I've ever had.

The spinach gets a little crispy on the sides and is still quite soft inside the fritter. The key to a crispy fritter is to keep the batter pretty dry and not water it down too much. Keep them warm in a low oven until you are ready to serve. I like to serve these with Tomato-Dal Soup (page 72) for a light meal.

SERVES 4–6

2 cups (80 g) packed fresh spinach leaves, washed and dried

1 large white onion, thinly sliced

½ cup (60 g) chickpea flour

2 tbsp (16 g) rice flour

½ tsp chili powder

⅓ tsp turmeric

¼ tsp salt

¼ tsp cumin seeds

⅓ cup (80 ml) water, or as needed

Vegetable oil, for frying

1 recipe Apple Cilantro Chutney (page 162), for serving

Chop up the spinach and add it to a mixing bowl. Add the onion, chickpea flour, rice flour, chili powder, turmeric, salt and cumin seeds. Using your hands, massage and mix everything well. The onion and spinach will wilt down a little bit and release their own juices. At this point add the water, 1 tablespoon (15 ml) at a time, and mix well. The batter should be lumpy and crumbly, not watery. You may need less than the ⅓ cup (80 ml).

Pour the oil to a depth of 3 to 4 inches (7.5 to 10 cm) into a deep pot or fryer and heat to 375°F (190°C) on a deep-frying thermometer.

Take about 1 tablespoon (15 g) of the onion-spinach mixture with your fingers or two spoons and carefully drop small nuggets into the oil. Do not crowd the pot. Let it fry for a minute or two, until crispy and golden brown, then turn and fry on the other side for a minute or two. Remove with a spider and place on a paper towel–lined plate to drain the excess oil. Repeat with the remaining batter, bringing the oil back up to temperature between batches. Serve with the chutney.

Note: Instead of deep-frying the fritters, you can panfry them. Just heat 2 to 3 tablespoons (30 to 45 ml) of oil in a skillet, drop some lumps of batter in and flatten with a spatula. Fry on both sides until well browned and serve.

MINCED LAMB CROQUETTES STUFFED WITH EGG

In India there's a wedding dish where a chicken is stuffed inside a goat and that chicken is stuffed with cooked eggs. The goat is cooked in a pit, covered with sand and charcoal. It's exotic and special.

My minced lamb croquettes are inspired by that dish. The surprise comes from the eggs, and I like the eggs diced and mixed with spices. I love hard-boiled eggs, but coating them with spices takes it to a whole other level. Serve with rice, naan and green chutney.

SERVES 4–6

LAMB

8 oz (227 g) minced lamb

5 cloves garlic, minced

¼ onion, grated

3 green chiles, grated

½ tsp Old Bay Seasoning

1 tsp garam masala

½ tsp freshly ground black pepper

1 tsp salt

STUFFING

4 hard-boiled eggs, finely diced

10 raisins

10 cashews, finely chopped

⅓ tsp salt

⅓ tsp freshly ground black pepper

3 tbsp (3 g) finely chopped cilantro

1 cup (120 g) fine semolina

¼ cup (60 ml) vegetable oil

To make the lamb, in a mixing bowl, combine the lamb, garlic, onion, green chiles, Old Bay, garam masala, pepper and salt. With clean hands, mix it gently to incorporate all the spices.

To make the stuffing, in another mixing bowl, combine the eggs, raisins, cashews, salt, pepper and cilantro and toss well with a spoon.

Take 2 tablespoons (30 g) of the lamb mixture and flatten it between your palms, then place 1 tablespoon (10 g) of the egg mixture in the center and slowly and carefully bring the sides together to make an oblong-shaped croquette. Spread the semolina on a plate and roll the croquette in the semolina to coat. Place the kebabs on a baking sheet, cover and refrigerate for at least 1 hour or up to 12 hours.

Preheat the oven to 400°F (200°C, or gas mark 6).

Remove the kebabs from the refrigerator, brush with the oil and bake for about 20 minutes, until they are brown and crisp and no pink remains in the center.

> **Note:** You can panfry these in some oil in a skillet instead of baking, if you prefer.

HASSELBACK EGG WITH CHILI AND FENNEL DRIZZLE

Yes, this might look simple, and yes, it is. But think about it—when a hard-boiled egg is thinly sliced, drizzled with a lot of love from the spiced oil and presented like this, it almost becomes the talk of the party. It goes from a plain old hard-boiled egg to "Hasselback eggs," with a sexy attitude. And all you did was slice the egg and drizzle it with some oil, but not any simple oil—flavored, amazing oil.

SERVES 4

4 large eggs

1⅓ tsp (8 g) salt, divided

3 tbsp (45 ml) olive oil

1 tsp brown mustard seeds

½ cumin seeds

⅓ tsp fennel seeds

Pinch of asafetida (optional)

6 cloves garlic, unpeeled and lightly crushed

½ tsp red chili powder

⅓ tsp turmeric

2 tbsp (2 g) finely chopped fresh cilantro, plus more for garnish

Gently place the eggs in a small saucepan, add cold water to cover and add 1 teaspoon of the salt. Bring the water to a boil, cover the pan and simmer for 3 minutes. Turn off the heat and let sit for 10 minutes. Drain the water and let the eggs cool before you peel them. Peel and set aside.

Make 5 to 6 cuts in the egg without going through it fully. The egg should still maintain the shape with the slits. If it helps, put a skewer horizontally through the bottom of the egg. Leave the skewer in until you are ready to serve.

Heat a small pan over medium heat and add the olive oil. Let it get hot and then add the mustard seeds, cumin seeds, fennel seeds, asafetida (if using) and garlic. After it splutters and calms, quickly add the red chili powder, turmeric and chopped cilantro. Sauté and cook over low heat for 30 seconds and then turn off the heat and add the remaining ⅓ teaspoon salt. Let the oil sit and soak in all the flavors for at least 15 to 30 minutes. Drizzle 1 teaspoon of the mixture over the cut eggs.

Note: Serve the eggs as a side for rice, on some pasta or just as a healthy snack.

MASALA CHICKEN WINGS

I was surprised by this recipe, and you will be, too. It is one of the most requested by my boys and one of the most popular ones on my blog. These wings have been featured in many places, and one of my favorite compliments came from Tyler Florence, chef and host of shows on the Food Network, who happens to love this recipe. It is quite straightforward and quick. You can prepare the sauce ahead and marinate the chicken the night before. All you have to do is bake and then dunk them in the sauce. The whole point of this dish is the combination of the garam masala, chiles and garlic, with some sweetness from pineapple juice. A mix of green chiles and black pepper really brings out the dimensions in the heat levels, so use both, though you can reduce or increase the amounts, as you wish.

SERVES 4–6

2 tbsp (20 g) ginger garlic paste

2 tbsp (30 ml) low-sodium soy sauce

2 lb (908 g) chicken wings

SAUCE

1 tsp vegetable oil

10 cloves garlic, very thinly sliced

5 green chiles, or to taste, thinly sliced

½ tsp garam masala

2 tsp (10 ml) low-sodium soy sauce

1 tbsp (15 ml) chili sauce (I use Maggi Hot & Sweet sauce)

1 tbsp (14 g) ketchup

½ cup (120 ml) fresh pineapple or orange juice (no canned stuff)

1 tsp cornstarch

Salt

½ tsp freshly ground black pepper

1 scallion, finely chopped

1 tbsp (1 g) finely chopped cilantro

Combine the ginger garlic paste and soy sauce in a large bowl and stir with a fork to blend. Add the chicken wings and toss in the sauce to coat. Cover with plastic wrap and marinate in the refrigerator overnight, or for at least 2 hours.

Preheat the oven at 400°F (200°C, or gas mark 6). Line a baking sheet with foil and top with a cooling rack.

Spread the marinated chicken wings in one layer on the rack and bake for 20 minutes, or until crispy. You can baste the chicken with the marinade once during cooking.

To make the sauce, heat the oil in a sauté pan over very low heat. Add the sliced garlic and green chiles and fry for 2 minutes. Then add the garam masala, soy sauce, chili sauce and ketchup and stir to combine. In a small cup, stir the pineapple juice and cornstarch very well, add it to the pan and stir continuously. Once it thickens and has a good consistency, turn off the heat and taste for salt. Add the black pepper and scallion.

Add the cooked chicken to the pan while the sauce is still hot and toss well. Serve immediately, sprinkled with the cilantro.

CHAPTER 3

VEGETARIAN MAINS

Me: "Lunch will be served in 10 minutes."

Little One: (excited) "Mum, it smells so good. Is it chicken?"

Me: (almost worried) "No. It's not chicken, hon."

Little One: "Mom, not again, not vegetarian."

Me: "It's a pita wrap, you might like it."

Little One: (sighing) "Okay, fine."

I bring the wraps to the table, and everyone starts lunch. The little boy eats in silence, with a tiny drip of yogurt sauce in the corner of his mouth. He exclaims, "This is the best vegetarian meal ever." His bright eyes and smile make me happy.

I get absolutely amazed glances when I say I prefer vegetarianism. "But you cook meat so much!" Yes, I do, for my meat-loving family. I think Indian vegetarian food has so much to offer, so much variety, so many flavors and textures, without it being boring or mundane. And how astounded some people are when they come for dinner or I take a vegetarian dish over and it is delicious and they want seconds. My favorites are vegan Chickpea Cauliflower Stew with Apple and Onion Salad (page 75), Potato and Chickpea Burger with Apple Cilantro Chutney (page 76), and Sweet Potato and Paneer Galette (page 78). I often have meat eaters digging in to a vegetarian curry or chickpea patty and saying, with complete astonishment, "But this is good."

So this chapter is dedicated to my vegetarian lovers. You can make them for two, three or four people, or for a huge party. Every single recipe is made with bold flavors and perfect for entertaining.

SPICED CHICKPEA PANCAKE (SOCCA)

This is a wonderfully simple dish that is so hearty. This is, in fact, a snack-time dish, but add vegetables and it makes a nice light lunch. I love how you can tailor this dish to your own tastes by adding any stuffing to it.

SERVES 4

PANCAKES

1 cup (120 g) chickpea flour

1 cup (235 ml) water, at room temperature

3 tbsp (45 ml) olive oil

4 scallions, finely chopped

2 tbsp (2 g) finely chopped cilantro

¼ tsp sea salt

⅓ tsp freshly ground black pepper

¼ cup (60 ml) vegetable oil, divided, for frying

TOPPING

2 cups (280 g) cubed squash

1 tsp grated ginger

½ tsp ground coriander

1 tsp chili powder

¼ tsp dry mango powder

1 tsp sugar

½ tsp salt

2 tsp (10 ml) olive oil

¼ cup (38 g) crumbled feta

Handful of baby greens

2 tbsp (12 g) finely chopped sun-dried tomatoes (either oil-packed or not)

Extra virgin olive oil, for drizzling

To make the pancakes, in a mixing bowl, combine the chickpea flour, water, olive oil, scallions, cilantro, salt and pepper. Whisk until smooth. Use immediately, or cover and let stand at room temperature for 30 minutes to 2 hours, or refrigerate overnight.

To make the topping, preheat the oven to 400°F (200°C, or gas mark 6).

In a large bowl, combine the squash, ginger, coriander, chili powder, mango powder, sugar, salt and oil. Toss well to coat, spread on a baking sheet and bake for 10 to 15 minutes, until fork tender. Remove from the oven and set aside.

Heat a 7- or 9-inch (18- or 23-cm) nonstick or cast-iron skillet over medium heat. Once it gets hot, add 1 tablespoon (15 ml) of the vegetable oil and 2 ladlefuls of the batter; cover and cook for 2 minutes on one side. Then flip, decrease the heat to medium-low and cook for another 2 minutes, until brown and crisp on the sides. Remove from the skillet and keep warm in a low oven while you repeat with the remaining batter and oil to make 3 more pancakes.

Serve the pancakes topped with the squash cubes, crumbled feta, baby greens, sun-dried tomatoes and a drizzle of extra virgin olive oil.

THREE BEAN SALAD WITH BOILED PEANUTS

I call this my Buddha salad. While this chickpea salad reminds me of festivals, it reminds many people of the food that they find on Indian beaches. Vendors carrying cane baskets shout out the name of the dish, and wrap the warm salad neatly in recycled newspaper for customers.

I always come back to what my mom makes, what I consider the best chickpea salad. She is generous with the peanuts and the coconut. I like to add a few more beans, for the color and to make a heartier dish. This is eaten at room temperature and makes a great light lunch.

SERVES 4–6

---

1 cup (120 g) green mung beans

½ cup (95 g) split yellow mung beans

1 tbsp (15 ml) canola oil

1 tsp mustard seeds

1 tsp cumin seeds

10 curry leaves

3 red chiles, broken in half

1 red onion, finely diced

½ tsp salt, divided

1 (15-oz [420-g]) can chickpeas, drained and rinsed very well

1 cucumber, seeded and diced

⅓ cup (25 g) freshly grated or frozen (unsweetened) coconut

¼ cup (37 g) raw peanuts, cooked in salted water for 10 minutes

½ tsp lemon juice

Soak the green mung beans in cold water overnight, drain very well, put in a box with some paper towels and cover. Refrigerate the beans for a couple of days until you see the sprouts. Alternatively, you can soak the green mung beans in water for 4 hours and then boil in fresh water for 10 minutes to get the rawness out. You can even eat the sprouted mung beans raw. Set aside.

Soak the split yellow mung beans in cold water for 1 hour, drain and set aside.

In a nonstick flat-bottomed pan, heat the oil over medium heat. Once the oil gets hot, add the mustard seeds, cumin seeds, curry leaves and red chiles and sauté for 1 minute. Don't let the red chiles get dark. Add the onion and ¼ teaspoon of the salt and sauté for just a minute. Add the chickpeas, green mung beans and split yellow mung beans and toss very well. Check for seasoning. Turn off the heat, add the cucumber, coconut, remaining ¼ teaspoon salt and salted boiled peanuts and stir to combine. Squeeze some lemon juice over the whole salad before serving warm.

GRILLED BOK CHOY AND SRIRACHA CHICKPEAS WITH BUTTERMILK DRESSING

I remember how this dish came to be. I found these beautiful bok choy and I got them home, not knowing how to cook them or what they would taste like. I called out to my teenage son to search for a recipe with bok choy. The first thing he found was a grilled bok choy recipe. I had some chickpeas, and so we grilled the bok choy, I quickly whipped up a buttermilk dressing and we tossed the whole thing together. Often, the grocery store gives me tons of ideas for trying new vegetables and a lot of times we fall in love with it. This is definitely one of those vegetables I have fallen in love with. If you can't find bok choy, you can substitute collard greens, Swiss chard or even beet greens.

SERVES 4

SALAD

1 (15-oz [420-g]) can chickpeas, drained, rinsed well and dried on a paper towel

3 tbsp (27 g) cornmeal, more if needed

2 tbsp (16 g) chickpea flour

3 tbsp (45 ml) Sriracha

½ tsp chaat masala

2 tbsp (30 ml) olive oil, plus more for drizzling

4 heads bok choy

Salt and pepper to taste

BUTTERMILK DRESSING

½ cup (120 ml) buttermilk

2 cloves garlic, grated

1 tbsp (11 g) home-style mustard

1 tbsp (20 g) honey

Salt and pepper to taste

Preheat the oven to 425°F (220°C, or gas mark 7) for 15 minutes. Line a baking sheet with parchment paper.

To make the salad, in a large mixing bowl, combine the chickpeas, cornmeal, chickpea flour, Sriracha, chaat masala and oil and toss well to coat all the chickpeas. Add more cornmeal if needed so the chickpeas are dry and well coated. Spread the chickpeas in a single layer on the prepared baking sheet and bake for 20 to 30 minutes, or until lightly crispy. Remove from the oven and let cool before using. Turn the oven down to 350°F (180°C, or gas mark 4).

Cut the bok choy heads in half and place on a separate baking sheet. Drizzle with some oil and sprinkle with salt and pepper. Bake or grill for 5 minutes. Alternatively, you can just wilt the bok choy in a nonstick pan or stove top griddle.

To make the dressing, mix all the ingredients in a small bowl and refrigerate until ready to use.

You can serve the bok choy in halves, arranging them on a platter, or dice them up and toss with the chickpeas. Either way, add the buttermilk dressing to the bowl with the chickpeas. Serve warm.

TOMATO-DAL SOUP

This is my "simple dal soup," which just got a makeover. Give me soup, even when I'm sick and I'll cringe. Add some fritters to it and I'll enjoy it happily. Even as a kid I wanted to fancy up the simplest dishes.

I tried to keep the authentic flavors of the most popular South Indian everyday dal but added my own twist. This is my homage to my simple heritage and our simple food. The tomatoes are cooked with the lentils, making them soft and sweet. It comes together quite quickly. The spinach fritters are a special touch. Serve the soup with some plain rice or just as is; it is sure to be a regular at your table.

SERVES 4

½ cup pigeon peas or yellow lentils (toovar or toor dal), washed and soaked for 30 minutes

3 large plum tomatoes, halved

1 sprig cilantro

2 hot red chiles

1 tsp salt

⅓ tsp plus ¼ tsp turmeric, divided

4 cups (940 ml) water

1 tbsp (14 g) ghee

1 tsp black mustard seeds

⅓ tsp asafetida powder

1 tsp tamarind paste or ⅓ cup (80 ml) tamarind water from a fresh tamarind block

1 tsp cumin seeds

1 tsp whole black pepper

2 tbsp (2 g) finely chopped cilantro

12–16 Spinach Fritters (page 58)

Use a pressure cooker or a soup pot (the latter will take much longer). In a pressure cooker, combine the pigeon peas, tomatoes, cilantro, red chiles, salt, ⅓ teaspoon of the turmeric and the water. Cover, bring to a boil over medium-high heat, put on the whistle, reduce the heat to medium-low and let it boil and cook for 4 whistles, or about 20 minutes. Turn off the heat and let the pressure go down for about 20 minutes. To use a soup pot, add the ingredients and simmer for 1 to 2 hours until soft.

In the meantime, place a small sauté pan over medium heat. Add the ghee, let it gets lightly hot, making sure not to let it brown too much, and then add the mustard seeds, remaining ¼ teaspoon turmeric and asafetida powder. Let the mustard seeds splutter and then add the tamarind paste or water. Turn off the heat and set aside.

Open the pressure cooker lid when the pressure is completely gone. When the dal is completely cooled down, carefully mash or puree the tomato and dal mixture very well in a countertop blender or with an immersion blender. Strain the soup through a fine-mesh strainer or cheesecloth into a clean pot. Toss the tomato peel and what remains in the cheesecloth or strainer. Add the ghee mixture to the soup and mix well.

In a separate small pan, combine the cumin seeds and peppercorn and dry roast, shaking the pan often, until you smell the spices. Transfer to a spice grinder or mortar and pestle and grind to a fine powder. Add to the soup and mix well. Sprinkle the soup with the cilantro and serve with the fritters.

CHICKPEA CAULIFLOWER STEW WITH APPLE AND ONION SALAD

Sometimes you make something and wonder how you created that miraculous flavor. My food sisters would vouch for this dish. I remember them telling me, "Put this in your book," and I said, "Yes, my darlings." I surprise myself with this dish even now. Is it the spices that make it so good, or just the combination of ingredients? In my opinion, the combination of the banana squash, chickpeas and cauliflower just works. If you can't find banana squash, you can substitute it with sugar pumpkin, buttercup squash, kabocha squash or even acorn squash. The final effect is a hearty dish with a fresh, light touch from the apple and onion salad. Serve with Fried Banana Bread (page 33), rice, roti or bread.

SERVES 4–6

2 tbsp (30 ml) vegetable oil

1 tsp cumin seeds

1 red onion, finely chopped

1 tbsp (10 g) ginger garlic paste

1 large ripe tomato, chopped

1 tsp salt

2 cups (280 g) peeled and diced banana squash

1 head cauliflower, cut into 2" (5-cm) pieces

¼ tsp turmeric

1½ cups (355 ml) water, divided

1 cup (235 ml) light coconut milk

1 (15-oz [420-g]) can chickpeas, drained and rinsed

3–4 green chiles or 1 tsp chili powder

½ tsp garam masala

Chopped cilantro, for garnish

APPLE AND ONION SALAD

1 Gala apple, unpeeled, cut into long, thin strips

½ onion, thinly sliced

Pinch of salt

½ tsp lemon juice

Add the oil to a deep pot over medium heat and let it get hot. Add the cumin and let it toast for 20 seconds, being careful not to burn it. Add the red onion and let it sweat and get light golden brown, 1 minute. Add the ginger garlic paste, turn the heat to low and fry for a minute. Add the tomato and salt and sauté until they are soft and disintegrated, 2 minutes.

Add the squash, cauliflower, turmeric and ½ cup (120 ml) of the water and cook, uncovered, for 2 minutes or until the cauliflower is 50 percent cooked but still crisp. Add the coconut milk, chickpeas, green chiles, garam masala and remaining 1 cup (235 ml) water and simmer for 5 to 7 minutes, until the cauliflower is cooked, yet keeping it crunchy. Turn off the heat.

To make the salad, combine the ingredients in a small bowl. Serve the stew with the salad and sprinkle with cilantro.

POTATO AND CHICKPEA BURGER WITH APPLE CILANTRO CHUTNEY

Also known as vada pav, this vegetarian burger is one of India's most popular street foods. I would go so far as saying that it is one of the most liked foods by Indians and many others around the world. There is so much depth of flavor in chaat, which is just a collection of dishes that are sold on the streets and in small shops. The potato burger is dipped in a thick chickpea batter and deep-fried. Stuffed in a soft roll, it is doused with chutney to intensify what already is pretty perfect. The stuffing is a traditional one, and making sure it is quite dry will give you good final results.

MAKES 4 BURGERS

BURGERS

4 large Yukon gold potatoes

2 green chilies, finely chopped

3 tbsp (3 g) finely chopped cilantro

½ tsp salt

⅓ tsp turmeric

COATING

1 cup (120 g) chickpea flour

½ tsp chili powder

⅓ tsp turmeric

⅓ tsp garam masala

⅓ tsp salt

½–1 cup (120–235 ml) water

1 cup (235 ml) vegetable oil, for frying

FOR SERVING

4 Peppery Cumin Buns (page 30)

1 recipe Apple Cilantro Chutney (page 162)

Watercress

To make the burgers, wash and scrub the potatoes very well. Put in a pot of cold water, bring to a boil over medium-high heat, cover and cook for 10 to 12 minutes, or until the potatoes are fork tender. Turn off the heat, drain the potatoes immediately and let cool. Once they are cool and there's no water retained in the potatoes, peel and mash them. Add them to a bowl, add the green chilies, cilantro, salt and turmeric and mix well. Form into 4 uniform patties 4 to 5 inches (10 to 13 cm) wide and ½ to 1 inch (1.3 to 2.5 cm) thick and set aside.

To make the coating, in a bowl, combine the chickpea flour, chili powder, turmeric, garam masala and salt. Add the water, ⅓ cup (80 ml) at a time, until a thick pancake-like batter forms.

Heat the oil in a skillet over medium-high heat oil and let it get hot. Dip each potato patty into the chickpea batter uniformly on all sides and carefully slide it into the oil. Cook until the chickpea batter is crispy, golden brown, about 2 minutes, then flip and cook on the other side until crispy and golden brown. Remove to a rack and set aside until ready to assemble the burgers. Repeat with the remaining patties.

To serve, cut the burger buns in half, spread 1 teaspoon of chutney on the bottom half of the bun, top it with the potato chickpea patty, add some watercress and more chutney and then replace the top of the burger bun. Serve warm.

SWEET POTATO AND PANEER GALETTE

If you like samosas, you will love this. It's a rustic and glorious pastry that is so good as a snack, or serve it with a green salad for a fancy, yet easy, lunch. The best part is, it tastes amazing at room temperature. Imagine taking this to a small romantic picnic, with some wine and fresh fruits . . . I might just do that this weekend.

SERVES 6

DOUGH

1⅓ cups (160 g) all-purpose flour

1 tsp sugar

⅓ tsp ajwain or caraway seeds

½ tsp fine sea salt

1 large egg

½ cup (112 g) unsalted butter, cut into large pieces

2 tsp (10 ml) lemon juice

½ tsp grated lemon zest (optional)

FILLING

2 tbsp (30 ml) olive oil

½ tsp cumin seeds

1 small red onion, finely chopped

½ tsp ginger garlic paste

2–3 Thai green chiles, finely chopped

1 small sweet potato, peeled and finely diced

2 cups (300 g) soft crumbly paneer, Indian cottage cheese or feta cheese

1 tbsp (15 g) tomato paste

½ tsp sea salt

½ tsp garam masala

½ tsp red pepper flakes

½ tsp Italian seasoning

2 tbsp (2 g) finely chopped cilantro

1 tbsp (15 ml) heavy whipping cream, plus more for brushing

To make the dough, in a food processor fitted with a steel blade, or in a large bowl, pulse or mix together the flour, sugar, ajwain seeds and salt. In a measuring cup, lightly beat the egg and set it aside. Add the butter to the processor, or use a fork to break it up into pea-sized pieces; if using a food processor, do not overprocess. Drizzle the egg mixture over the dough and pulse or stir until it just starts to come together but is still mostly large crumbs. Mix in the lemon juice and lemon zest, if using. Transfer the dough to a lightly floured surface and pat it together to make a ball. Flatten into a disk, wrap in plastic and chill for 2 hours, or up to 3 days.

To make the filling, place a large, flat-bottomed nonstick pan over medium heat. After it gets hot, add the oil and then the cumin seeds. Let them pop for a few seconds and then add the chopped red onion and sauté until translucent, 3 to 4 minutes. Add the ginger garlic paste and green chiles and sauté for 30 seconds, and then add the sweet potato. Keep sautéing until the potato is browned and cooked well, 2 to 3 minutes. Then add the paneer and mix well. Use a spatula to break it up until it looks like mince. Alternatively, you can add the paneer to the food processor to break it into bits before adding it to the pan. Add the tomato paste, salt, garam masala, red pepper flakes and Italian seasoning and mix very well. Keep tossing until everything is incorporated and then add the cilantro and heavy whipping cream. Turn off the heat and let the mixture cool completely before moving on to the next step.

Preheat the oven to 400°F (20°C, or gas mark 6). Line a rimmed baking sheet with parchment paper. Take the chilled dough from the refrigerator and roll it out into a 12-inch (30-cm) round (it can be messy). Transfer to the prepared baking sheet and chill again for 30 minutes. Remove the dough from the refrigerator and pile the paneer mixture in the middle, leaving a 2-inch (5-cm) border. Gently fold the edges over the mixture, neatly pleat and brush with whipping cream. Bake for 35 to 45 minutes, or until the edges are golden brown. Remove from the oven and let cool for 20 minutes before serving.

PIZZA POCKETS WITH SPICED ASPARAGUS

I'm not too experimental with produce—well, I wasn't for a long time. The blog opened up my eyes to so many pretty vegetables and fruits. The best part about living in San Francisco is the easy access to a variety of fresh produce. Asparagus is versatile and adapts to its surroundings, but the best way to enjoy asparagus it to keep it simple. I find that the crunch is key to a tasty dish. Toss them lightly with spices and cook for few minutes. I adore the tiny heads peaking through the pizza pockets in this dish. A tasty quick treat would be to stuff this in puff pastry, too.

MAKES 6–8

1 tbsp (15 ml) olive oil

1 tsp cumin seeds

5 cloves garlic, thinly sliced

2 bunches asparagus, tough ends trimmed, cut into 1" (2.5-cm) pieces

2 tbsp (30 ml) water

1½ tsp (7 g) chili powder or smoked paprika

½ tsp salt

1 tsp lemon juice

1 (13.5-oz [378-g]) package store-bought pizza dough

½ cup (120 g) Onion Tomato Chutney (page 168)

1 egg, beaten (for egg wash)

⅓ cup (35 g) grated Parmesan cheese

Preheat the oven to 400°F (200°C, or gas mark 6). Line a baking sheet with parchment paper.

Heat a large nonstick skillet over medium-high heat. Add the oil and let it get hot. Add the cumin seeds and let them pop. Add the garlic, asparagus and water; cook, stirring often, for 3 minutes. Add the chili powder and salt and cook until the asparagus is still crisp, about 1 minute. Remove from the heat, add the lemon juice and set aside.

Roll out the pizza dough on a lightly floured surface to a thin 12 x 20-inch (30 x 52-cm) rectangle. Cut the rectangle in half lengthwise. Then cut each half into 8 equal rectangles.

Spread a teaspoon of the chutney on each rectangle, place 4 to 5 asparagus pieces in the middle, bring the ends together and pinch the sides or use a fork to seal and crimp the edges. Place the pizza pockets onto the prepared baking sheet. Brush the top of each pizza pocket with the egg wash and sprinkle with some Parmesan.

Bake until golden, 15 to 17 minutes.

SPICED LENTILS WITH SCALLOPED SWEET POTATO AND YAM

This dish takes no time to make and once you bring it to the table, it's going to get a standing ovation. The sweet chana dal, the soft, creamy split red dal and the nutty flat brown lentil all make a good combination. You can top this with any root vegetable you want, but try to keep it as thin as possible, so that it cooks and crisps up fast. I like serving it with flatbread, or if you want to go grain free, it's also great on its own.

SERVES 4–6

1 cup (190 g) flat brown lentils

½ cup (95 g) split red dal

⅓ cup (65 g) chana dal

2 cups (470 ml) water

⅔ tsp turmeric, divided

Salt

1 tbsp (15 ml) vegetable oil

10 curry leaves (optional)

½ tsp mustard seeds

½ tsp cumin seeds

Pinch of asafetida

½ tsp cayenne pepper or red chili powder

1 onion, diced or thinly sliced

4 cloves garlic, thinly sliced

½" (1.3-cm) piece ginger, peeled and minced

2 serrano chiles, finely sliced (seeded for less spice)

2 carrots, peeled and grated

2 medium tomatoes, diced

1 sweet potato, peeled

1 yam, peeled

1 tbsp (15 ml) olive oil

Pinch of red chili pepper

Salt and pepper

Handful of finely chopped cilantro

Wash the lentils and dals very well under running cold water until the water runs clear. Soak for 30 minutes in water to cover and then drain and set aside.

Preheat the oven to 400°F (200°C, or gas mark 6) for 15 minutes.

In a saucepan, combine the lentils, dals, water and ⅓ teaspoon of the turmeric and bring to a boil over medium-high heat; lower the heat to medium and cook, uncovered, for 5 minutes. Skim off the white foam that forms on top. Do not add salt at this point or it will toughen the lentils. Cover the pan and cook for 20 minutes longer, until the lentils are tender but still keep their shape. Turn off the heat, add salt to taste and set aside.

Heat the vegetable oil in a skillet over medium-high heat. Add the curry leaves if using, mustard seeds, cumin seeds and asafetida and let the seeds burst a bit. Immediately reduce the heat and add the remaining ⅓ teaspoon turmeric and the cayenne. Cook for 30 seconds and then add the onion, garlic, ginger and chiles and sauté until the onions are slightly brown, 1 minute, being careful not to burn the garlic. Add the carrots and tomatoes. Cook, stirring constantly, until the tomatoes have broken down and everything is cooked together, about 3 minutes. Then add the cooked lentils, bring it to a boil, turn off the heat and transfer to a 10-inch (25-cm) baking dish or any dish that will hold the lentils.

Thinly slice the sweet potato and yam and arrange them neatly over the lentils. Drizzle the olive oil evenly over the potatoes and sprinkle the chili pepper, salt and pepper. Bake for 15 minutes, or until the potatoes have cooked through. You can turn on the broiler for 5 minutes to brown the edges of the potatoes if you want. Serve immediately, sprinkled with cilantro.

STUFFED TOMATOES WITH TOFU SCRAMBLE AND EDAMAME

The juicy, sweet tomatoes of California are definitely the inspiration for this dish. Summers are my favorite time to make this. Although I am not big into gardening, my little one is. He was promised that he could adopt a dog if he grew forty tomatoes. To our utter shock, he did. I made a variety of stuffed tomatoes that summer, but he didn't get his dog for the next year or so. He took to gardening, and now he loves having a small vegetable patch, but his dog eats it up before it even has time to say hello to the world.

This is a pretty simple dish. Add any kind of grain you have on hand. I've used brown rice, black rice and sometimes semolina. I like a strong cheese for this, but if you can't find Pecorino, use feta instead. Both are equally delicious.

SERVES 4–6

8–10 Roma tomatoes, not too ripe

Kosher salt and freshly ground black pepper, to taste

2 tbsp (30 ml) olive oil, plus more for drizzling, divided

½ medium red onion, finely chopped

1 cup (150 g) shelled edamame

½ cup (75 g) crumbled soft tofu

½ cup (70 g) chopped green bell pepper

1 tsp minced garlic

1 tsp minced ginger

1 tsp green chile paste or ½ tsp red pepper flakes

½ tsp garam masala

½ cup (95 g) cooked quinoa

⅓ cup (6 g) chopped cilantro leaves

⅓ cup (35 g) grated Pecorino Romano

Preheat the oven to 350°F (180°C, or gas mark 4).

Cut the tops off the tomatoes. Using a spoon, remove the pulp and seeds and reserve for another recipe. Arrange the tomatoes in a 10-inch (25-cm) baking dish with tall sides. Sprinkle with salt and pepper and set aside.

Heat the oil in a large nonstick pan over medium heat. When it gets hot, add the onion and edamame and let it brown for a minute. Then crumble in the tofu and add the bell pepper. Cook for 2 to 3 minutes, or until browned a bit. Then add the garlic, ginger, green chile paste and salt it lightly. Keep stirring for another 5 to 6 minutes, until it's cooked fully. Add the garam masala, a good twist of fresh pepper, the quinoa and the cilantro and mix well.

Stuff the mixture into the prepared tomatoes, drizzle with some olive oil and sprinkle with the cheese. Bake, uncovered, for 20 minutes, or until the tomatoes are blistered but still hold their shape.

Notes: You can use vine-ripened tomatoes instead of Roma tomatoes and you can use paneer instead of tofu. Instead of quinoa, you can add some cooked brown rice or wild rice.

PITA WRAPS WITH CHAAT MASALA–SPICED KIDNEY BEANS AND SWEET POTATO AND JICAMA-MANGO SALAD

When a ten-year-old exclaims that this is the best vegetarian dish I've made, I knew I had to share it with the world. Though unorthodox, it is a great way to use red kidney beans. And the crunch and sweetness from the jicama and mango salad is addictive. I could eat a couple of these and feel good about it, too.

SERVES 4–6

FILLING

2 sweet potatoes, peeled

1 tbsp (15 ml) olive oil

1 tsp cumin seeds

½ tsp chaat masala

⅓ tsp chili powder

½ tsp salt

⅓ tsp sugar

1 cup (250 g) cooked red kidney beans

½ tbsp (8 ml) lime juice

SALAD

½ jicama, very thinly sliced to 2″ (5-cm) lengths

½ mango, pitted and thinly cut lengthwise

Juice of ½ orange (fresh juice is best)

1 tbsp (15 ml) olive oil

Salt and freshly ground pepper, to taste

Pinch of chili powder

YOGURT SAUCE

⅓ cup (80 g) full-fat yogurt

⅓ tsp salt

1 tsp chopped fresh mint

⅓ tsp sugar

FOR SERVING

4 pita bread

Peppery greens

To make the filling, cut the sweet potato in half, cut into long strips like fries and then dice them. The pieces should be the size of a red kidney bean; we want to keep everything the same size so it can cook evenly. Set aside.

Heat a large, flat-bottomed nonstick pan over medium heat. Add the olive oil and let it get hot. Add the cumin seeds and let them brown for a minute and then add the sweet potatoes. Toss to combine and sauté for about 3 minutes; once the potatoes are 70 percent cooked, add the chaat masala, chili powder, salt and sugar, turn the heat to medium-low and cook, tossing occasionally, until fully cooked, 3 to 4 minutes longer. Add the red kidney beans and toss well. Turn off the heat, add the lime juice and set aside.

To make the salad, place the jicama and mango in a bowl. In a separate bowl, combine the orange juice, olive oil, salt and pepper to taste and chili powder and mix well. Pour over the jicama and mango, toss gently and let sit for 5 minutes.

To make the yogurt sauce, combine all the ingredients in a small bowl. Chill in the refrigerator until you are ready to use it.

To serve, cut the pitas in half. Stuff each half with some peppery greens, then some sweet potato and bean filling and finally top with the jicama-mango salad. Drizzle with the yogurt sauce.

COCONUT RICE WITH PEAS

My South Indian heart cannot live without rice. One question I get asked a lot is how I get my rice so fluffy. And one of the things I am proud of is my ability to make it pretty perfectly. I'm not going to dwell on the days I forget to turn the stove off and rush to find a dark layer of crust on the bottom. On most days, the rice is perfectly fluffy and the each grain holds its shape.

The key to a good, fluffy rice is to first wash the rice well and then soak it in water for 30 minutes. The grains soak in enough liquid to hold their shape and create a good bond while cooking. If you soak the rice longer, the grains might break apart while cooking. The liquid ratio is key, too. To cook basmati or short-grain rice, use one part grain to two parts liquid. You will need more liquid for wild rice, black rice and brown rice. Simmer the rice for 20 minutes, turn off the heat and let it sit, covered, for 10 minutes. Letting it stand gives the rice enough time to soak up all the liquid and it gets fluffier.

SERVES 4

1 cup (165 g) Sona Masuri or any medium-grain, nonstarchy rice

1 tbsp (14 g) coconut oil

1 tbsp (15 ml) olive oil

1 tsp cumin seeds

1 bay leaf

1 star anise

½ cup (40 g) freshly grated or frozen coconut

3 mint leaves

2 green chiles, slit down the middle (remove seeds for less spice)

2 cups (470 ml) vegetable stock or water

Salt

1 cup (130 g) frozen sweet peas

Toasted cashews, for garnish

In a strainer, wash the rice under cold tap water until the water runs clear. Place in a bowl, cover with water and soak for 30 minutes.

In a medium-sized, heavy-bottomed pan over medium heat, add the coconut and olive oils and let it get lightly hot. Add the cumin seeds, bay leaf and star anise. Drain the rice and add it to the oil. Toss gently and sauté for 2 minutes; do not cook any longer or the rice grains will break. Add the grated coconut and toast over medium-low heat for 1 minute. Tear up the mint leaves and add them to the mixture along with the green chiles. Sauté for 1 minute.

In a separate pot, bring the vegetable stock to a boil, and then add it to the rice. Season with salt. Bring the rice to a boil, turn down the heat to medium, cover and simmer for 18 minutes. Turn off the heat and let sit for 15 minutes. Then add the sweet peas and cover again for 5 minutes. Fluff up the grains, add the toasted cashews and serve.

TOASTED FRUIT AND NUT WILD RICE

While white rice is delicious in its own way, wild rice is hearty and I absolutely love it. Toasting the rice before adding the spices and cooking with a slightly different technique gives it a unique twist.

SERVES 4

1 tbsp (15 ml) olive oil

1 cup (165 g) wild rice

1 tbsp (14 g) unsalted butter

1 tbsp (10 g) pine nuts

10 whole almonds

10 dried cranberries

15 light brown or dark raisins

½ red onion, chopped

5 cloves garlic, minced

½ tsp dried basil, crushed

½ tsp dried thyme, crushed

1 tsp flaky salt

½ tsp freshly ground black pepper

3 cups (705 ml) vegetable stock or water

Heat the olive oil in a pan over medium-low heat. Add the rice and toast for 2 minutes. Let cool, then add to a large pot with some water and wash the rice well, dumping out the old water and adding fresh water, until the water runs clear, at least 3 to 4 washes. Be gentle when you wash the rice, trying not to break the grains. Drain the last batch of water, cover with fresh water and let the rice soak for about 2 hours. Wild rice takes time to cook, so soaking is essential.

Place a saucepan or heavy-bottomed pan over medium heat. Add the butter, let it melt and then add the pine nuts, almonds, cranberries and raisins. Turn the heat to low and sauté for 1 minute, until toasted. Don't let the raisins burn or they will get bitter. Then add the onion and garlic and sauté until softened, 2 minutes. Add the basil, thyme, salt and black pepper. Add the liquid and bring it to a boil.

Drain the rice from the water it was soaking in and add the rice to the stock mixture. Bring it to a boil, lower the heat to a simmer and cook for 45 minutes. Turn off the heat and let it sit for another 10 minutes before uncovering the pot and fluffing the rice.

LENTIL-RICE RISOTTO WITH RAINBOW CHARD AND CRISPY CARROTS

Naming this dish was a challenge. I was inspired by a couple of my favorite rice dishes, the very popular risotto and a popular South Indian dish called pongal. It's a one-pot meal you can make in your pressure cooker, rice cooker or slow cooker. It is very crucial to keep it soft and add enough water, more than you think you need. Don't stir or mix it a lot so the rice grains will hold their shape. Curry leaves are very integral to this, but if you can't find them, don't worry. It will still be tasty. This dish is best eaten hot. It congeals as it cools and is not as pleasing to the senses.

SERVES 4

½ cup (95 g) yellow split mung dal

1 tbsp (15 ml) plus 1 tsp (5 ml) vegetable oil, divided

1 cup (165 g) short-grain rice (I use Sona Masuri from Indian stores or Arborio), washed and drained

5 cups (1175 ml) water or vegetable stock, divided

½ tsp plus ⅓ tsp salt, divided

2" (5-cm) piece ginger, thinly sliced

1 tsp coarsely ground black pepper

1 tsp cumin seeds

10 cashews, broken into pieces

10 curry leaves (optional, but makes a huge difference)

Pinch of asafetida

1 cup (50 g) chopped, packed rainbow chard

GARNISH

3 tbsp (45 ml) vegetable oil

2 carrots, peeled and cut into matchsticks

Place the yellow split mung dal in a pan over medium heat and stir, toasting lightly, for 2 minutes until it slightly turns color. Remove from the heat, wash very well in cold water and drain.

In large, heavy saucepan with 3-inch (7.5-cm) sides or a Dutch oven, heat 1 tablespoon (15 ml) of the vegetable oil over medium heat. Add the washed yellow dal and the rice and toast lightly again, being careful not to break the grains. Add 2 cups (470 ml) of the water, bring to a boil over medium-high heat and then turn down the heat to medium; cook, covered, without stirring, until all the water is absorbed, 20 minutes. Add the remaining 3 cups (705 ml) water, cover and cook over medium-low heat until the rice is completely cooked and softer in texture, about 30 minutes. Add ½ teaspoon of the salt, cover and turn off the heat.

In a sauté pan, heat the remaining 1 teaspoon of vegetable oil over medium heat. Add the ginger, pepper, cumin seeds, cashews, curry leaves (if using) and asafetida and fry until they splutter and become toasted, 30 seconds to 1 minute. Add the chopped rainbow chard and remaining ⅓ teaspoon salt and sauté until it is wilted down and cooked through, 4 to 5 minutes. Add the spicy chard mixture to the cooked rice mixture and stir to thoroughly combine. The rice should not be neither too firm nor soggy or watery. When you spoon it onto a plate, it should very slowly spread. Check for salt and turn off the heat.

For the garnish, heat the oil in a flat-bottomed, nonstick pan over medium-high heat. Add the chopped carrots and cook until caramelized and crispy, 2 minutes. Remove from the pan and drain on a paper towel.

Serve the risotto with the crispy carrots on top.

CHAPTER 4

EGGS, CHICKEN & SEAFOOD

We walked past the dirt and grime of the fresh seafood market, weaving our way through a swarm of people in the tiny, dark alley. Mini me held on for dear life at my grandma's *pallu* (the corner of her sari). The fishy smell irked me a bit. Just a few days later, she spoke to the man about how fresh the goat legs were. Chicken was a staple, nothing out of the ordinary for us then.

My knowledge of meat and seafood dishes was quite vast, although I didn't particularly enjoy them all. Our huge family loved nonvegetarian meals. Funny that my little man is exactly like his great-grandma. He will try everything, anything and thoroughly enjoy it.

Our Sunday lunch has always been special. My parents made it special for me, and I try to make it special for my boys. Lunch, followed by a nap and evening coffee with snacks, is a routine I don't mess around with.

We have our staple chicken dishes like our Harissa Roast Chicken with Rice and Eggs (page 119) and Tamarind Skillet Chicken (page 97). There are a few staple dishes that I've transformed to make my own, like the Eggplant Rollatini Stuffed with Minced Garlicky Fish (page 112); a momos (wonton) soup, which is like my mum's authentic Chicken Soup with Vegetable-Stuffed Wontons (page 108) and the black peppery Fish Tacos (page 116). There are classic dishes like the Curried Crab Corn Chowder (page 125) that I love adding curry powder to. It's a great, subtle spice, and adds so much depth to the coconut milk soup. These dishes are great for company or as an addition to party menus.

EGGS COOKED IN TOMATO AND TAMARIND SAUCE

This is a potent dish almost always served with rice, which goes well with the tamarind and the eggs. Every South Indian household has its own mix for curries, but a tamarind-based curry is almost always the same. Some people add okra to the curry, and mini eggplants are popular, but I've never seen eggs cooked like this. My mum made it once and I've been hooked on it ever since. It's a surprising twist on the traditional shakshuka.

SERVES 4

SAUCE

2 tomatoes

½ onion

2 Thai green chiles

3 cups (705 ml) water, divided

1 tbsp (15 ml) sesame oil

2 tbsp (30 ml) canola oil

1 tsp brown mustard seeds

1 tsp cumin seeds

10 curry leaves

Pinch of asafetida

10–20 cloves garlic, halved

1 tsp red chili powder, or to taste

½ tsp ground coriander

⅓ turmeric

1 tsp salt

½ cup (100 g) diluted tamarind pulp or 1 tbsp (14 g) tamarind paste

1 tbsp (12 g) brown sugar or 1 golf ball-sized piece of jaggery

4 large eggs

Steamed rice, for serving

To make the sauce, combine the tomatoes, onion, green chiles and 1 cup (235 ml) of the water in a blender and blend until smooth. Set aside.

In a heavy-bottomed saucepan, add the sesame oil and canola oil and place over medium heat. Once it gets mildly hot, add the mustard seeds, cumin seeds, curry leaves and asafetida. Be cautious at this point as the curry leaves will pop and the oil will splatter. Reduce the heat, toss in the garlic and sauté until it is slightly softened and golden brown, 1 minute. Add the tomato-onion paste gently to the oil mixture. Keep stirring. Add the red chili powder, coriander, turmeric and salt and stir over medium to low heat until it dries up and you see oil ooze out the sides.

Add the remaining 2 cups (470 ml) water and let it come to a boil, then add the tamarind juice, cover and cook for 15 minutes over medium heat. Remove the lid and let it reduce a bit. Check for salt. Add the brown sugar and stir to combine.

Reduce the heat to a simmer. Very carefully, break an egg into a small bowl, make a well in the sauce with the back of a spoon and add the egg to the well. Repeat to add all the eggs and simmer for 5 to 7 minutes, until the eggs are done to your liking. Remove from the heat and serve with some steamed rice.

*See photo on page 92.

WHITE CHICKEN CURRY POT PIE

This dish is deliciously simple and aesthetically pleasing. It is good baked in a large baking dish or served individually. It is rich and luxurious, which is why I like to serve it in individual-sized bakeware.

SERVES 4–6

2 lb (908 g) boneless chicken or 3 chicken breasts

2 large potatoes or 10 baby potatoes

2 carrots

3 cups (705 ml) water, divided

2 onions, quartered

10 cloves garlic

1" (2.5-cm) piece ginger

Small handful of cashew pieces

1 tsp cumin seeds

1 tsp coriander seeds

1" (2.5-cm) cinnamon stick

4 cloves

4 cardamom pods

1 star anise (optional)

2 bay leaves

2 tbsp (30 ml) vegetable oil

4 green chiles, slit slightly

Salt

½ cup (120 ml) semi-thick coconut milk, or more as needed

1 tsp white or black pepper

CRUST

1 sheet puff pastry, thawed

1 egg, beaten, or heavy cream

1 tbsp (8 g) black sesame seeds

Wash the chicken and cut into bite-sized pieces of about 1 inch (2.5 cm).

Peel the potatoes and dice them the same size as the chicken. If you plan on using baby potatoes, you don't need to peel, and just halve them. Dice the carrots the same size as the chicken.

In a saucepan, combine 2 cups (470 ml) of the water and the quartered onions, garlic, ginger and cashew pieces. Bring to a boil, lower the heat to a simmer and cook for about 15 minutes. Turn off the heat and let cool completely. Transfer the onion mixture to a blender and blend to a smooth paste.

Place the cumin seeds, coriander seeds, cinnamon, cloves, cardamom, star anise (if using) and bay leaves in a piece of cheesecloth and bring the corners up to make a bag; tie. Crush it ever so lightly with a knife or a garlic pounder.

Add the oil to a heavy-bottomed pan over medium heat and let it get hot. Add the spice sachet to the hot oil. Then add the onion mixture and simmer. Do not let the mixture get brown at all. Add the green chiles and the salt. Add the chicken pieces, potatoes, carrots and remaining 1 cup (235 ml) water. Cover and cook for about 20 minutes, or until the veggies are tender and the chicken is cooked through. Open the lid, add the coconut milk and pepper and simmer for another 5 minutes, or until the desired consistency is reached. If you like it thicker, boil uncovered for a few minutes longer; if you want it thinner, add little bit more coconut milk. Turn off the heat and let it cool.

Preheat the oven to 425°F (220°C, or gas mark 7). Spoon the chicken mixture into individual ramekins or a baking dish.

To make the crust, unroll the puff pastry and cut into any shape you want. Place on top of the chicken, brush with the egg wash and sprinkle with the sesame seeds. Bake for 10 to 15 minutes, until the crust is golden and the sauce is bubbling.

Note: Alternatively you can bake the puff pastry separately on a baking tray and top it on the chicken pot pie. I find that this way the puff pastry cooks through.

TAMARIND SKILLET CHICKEN

I absolutely love to cook some of my traditional dishes in a cast-iron pan, and many people say that food tastes so good cooked this way. I have to agree. Use only salt to wash the pan and take care good of it.

This is a two-step dish. Marinating the chicken helps to season it and keep it moist. Then adding it to the masala intensifies and makes it special. I recommend getting a block of tamarind and using fresh instead of the bottled paste, which is too concentrated and just too potent. You can even add the tamarind masala sauce to the yogurt mixture, marinate overnight and grill the chicken the next day.

SERVES 6

MARINADE

½ cup (120 g) thick full-fat yogurt

2 tbsp (28 g) ginger garlic paste

1 tsp chili powder

½ tsp turmeric

2 tbsp (30 ml) oil

2 tsp (12 g) salt

6 large chicken thighs

TAMARIND MASALA SAUCE

2 tbsp (10 g) coriander seeds

1 tbsp (6 g) cumin seeds

1 tsp peppercorns

½ tsp fenugreek seeds (meethi)

10–12 whole red chiles, to taste

2 tbsp (16 g) white sesame seeds

½ cup (100 g) thick tamarind pulp, or 2 tsp (9 g) tamarind paste mixed in ½ cup (120 ml) water

2 tbsp (30 ml) vegetable oil

10–15 pearl onions

⅓ cup (80 g) ketchup (I use Maggi Hot and Sweet sauce)

1 tbsp (14 g) tomato paste (optional)

1 tsp salt

Chopped fresh cilantro, for garnish

Lemon wedges, for garnish

To make the marinade, combine all the marinade ingredients in a large mixing bowl. Mix well. Add the chicken to the bowl, turn to coat, cover and let marinate in the refrigerator for at least 3 hours or overnight (overnight is best).

To make the sauce, toast the coriander seeds, cumin seeds, peppercorns, fenugreek seeds and whole red chiles in a skillet over low heat until you smell the spices, about 1 minute. Do not let the spices burn. Turn off the heat, add the sesame seeds to the hot pan and stir for a minute or two. Transfer to a blender along with the tamarind pulp and blend to a very smooth paste. Don't add any water.

Add the oil to a heavy-bottomed cast-iron skillet or *kadai* and let it get hot over high heat. Add the chicken with the marinade mix. Let it sear and cook and one side. After about 2 minutes, turn the chicken and sear it for another 3 minutes. Then add the pearl onions and toss and brown them. Add the sauce, ketchup, tomato paste and salt, cover the pan and cook the chicken over medium heat for 20 minutes until it is fork tender. Open and check if the chicken is completely cooked. Then uncover the pan and let it dry down until all the sauce sticks to the chicken, tossing occasionally. Serve garnished with some chopped cilantro and a drizzle of lemon juice.

Note: This dish tastes amazing served with herbed rice or Coconut Rice with Peas (page 86). Serve it with some naan and you have a dish to entertain with.

CHICKEN AND WAFFLES

This is soul food for Southerners—sweet, salty and crunchy—with my Indian twist. Quite a dynamic combo, they say. Chicken fried like this with chickpea flour is a favorite snack in India. Pair it with the savory waffle, top it with some sweet and sour yogurt and fresh onion and it is a delight. Waffles can be made with many grains. I like using semolina, which almost tastes like a upma or raw dosa mix.

SERVES 4–6

CHICKEN

3 boneless skinless chicken breasts, cut into 1″ (2.5-cm) strips, patted dry

3 tbsp (24 g) chickpea flour

1 tbsp (8 g) smooth rice flour

1 tsp cornstarch

2 tsp (4 g) chili powder, or to taste

1 tbsp (14 g) ginger garlic paste

1 egg, beaten

1 tsp salt, or to taste

Drop of red food coloring (optional)

Vegetable oil, for deep-frying

WAFFLES

2 cups (240 g) fine semolina

1 cup (140 g) cornmeal

2 large eggs

⅓ cup (80 g) plain thick yogurt

3 Thai green chiles, finely diced

1 large carrot, peeled and finely grated

1 tsp salt

⅓ tsp baking soda

⅓ tsp turmeric

3 tbsp (3 g) finely chopped cilantro

4 tbsp (56 g) unsalted butter, melted

1 recipe Yogurt Sauce (page 164)

Thinly sliced onion, for serving

To make the chicken, add the chicken pieces to a mixing bowl. Add the chickpea flour, rice flour, cornstarch, chili powder, ginger garlic paste, egg and salt. If you add the red food coloring, use a spoon so that you do not stain your hands. If you don't use the coloring, with clean hands, mix and toss everything to coat each chicken piece. Cover and marinate for at least 30 minutes on the countertop or overnight in the refrigerator.

Heat 1½ to 2 inches (3.8 to 5 cm) of vegetable oil in a deep skillet over medium-high heat until it reaches 365°F (185°C) on a deep-frying thermometer. Lower the heat slightly, if necessary, to keep the oil from getting hotter.

If you've marinated the chicken in the refrigerator, take it out and let it come to room temperature. Fry the chicken in small batches until crisp, 4 to 5 minutes. Remove from the oil and drain on paper towels.

To make the waffles, combine all the ingredients in a large bowl and set it on the countertop for 10 minutes. Preheat a waffle iron for 5 minutes. Brush the iron with some oil or spray with nonstick spray. Pour a large ladleful of batter, and cook for 2 minutes. Using tongs, take it out and keep warm in a low oven. Repeat to use all the waffle batter.

Serve a few chicken pieces over the warm waffles, drizzled with some yogurt sauce and topped with the onion.

CHICKEN MEATBALLS SAUTÉED WITH GARLIC AND HERBS

I probably make meatballs every week, in every combination imaginable, but the base is pretty much the same. I've made meatballs with fennel, with dill, with spinach, with veggies and I like to use turkey meat or minced lamb, but I prefer minced chicken and a little bit of fat from an egg; adding cream helps keep it juicy and moist. I also think grated onion adds the required moistness. People often ask me how I get perfectly round meatballs. I use a *paniyaram* or a Danish *aebleskiver* pan, which requires little oil and produces flawless round meatballs. But if you are not concerned about the perfect size, use a good heavy-bottomed pan to get the perfect crust. These meatballs are scrumptious either way.

MAKES 20–30 MEATBALLS

1 lb (454 g) minced chicken

Zest of 1 lemon

½ tsp sea salt, plus more to taste

2 slices white bread

2 tbsp (30 ml) heavy cream

1 egg

1 tsp (5 ml) plus 3 tbsp (45 ml) vegetable oil, divided

½ tsp black cumin seeds

3 green chiles chopped

½ onion, grated

1 tbsp (14 g) ginger garlic paste

⅓ tsp freshly ground black pepper

½ tsp garam masala

¼ tsp turmeric

Pinch of red pepper flakes

10 cloves garlic, thinly sliced

⅓ cup (6 g) finely chopped cilantro

1 tbsp (1 g) chives

1 tsp soy sauce

¼ tsp lemon juice

In a mixing bowl, combine the minced chicken, lemon zest and salt; toss to season the chicken.

In a separate bowl, add the bread and cream and let it soak well. Mash the bread mixture. Beat the egg and add it to the bread mixture; stir to combine. Set aside.

Heat 1 teaspoon of the oil in a sauté pan over medium heat. Add the black cumin seeds and green chiles and fry for 1 minute. Add the grated onion and ginger garlic paste and fry to get the raw flavor out, about 1 minute. Add salt to taste, remove from the heat and let cool.

Once it's completely cooled, add it to the chicken mixture along with the bread mixture, pepper, garam masala, turmeric, red pepper flakes and salt to taste. Using clean hands, mix gently. The mixture has to be dry; don't overwork it.

Place a flat-bottomed pan over medium heat and add the remaining 3 tablespoons (45 ml) oil. You can use a mini ice cream scoop or your hands to form the meatballs. Lightly oiling your hands, take 1 tablespoon (14 g) of the mixture and roll it make a smooth ball; place it gently in the pan. Fry the meatballs for 5 to 7 minutes, tossing a bit so that all the sides are browned evenly and cooked through. You can cover the pan for 2 to 3 minutes to steam cook it.

Remove the cover once the meatball is completely cooked through, add the garlic, cilantro and chives and toss very well. Add the soy sauce and toss for 15 seconds and turn off the heat. Add the lemon juice and serve immediately.

CHICKEN MEATBALLS AND NOODLES IN SPICY PLUM BARBECUE SAUCE

When I first made this barbecue sauce after a visit to Ardenwood Historic Farm, where we bought bags of plum for pennies, I put it on everything. That plum barbecue sauce has to be bottled, said my friend. I've made many bottles and batches of this to share and it is by far one of my favorite summer sauces. Brush it on tofu, paneer or lamb chops or toss it with chicken meatballs and noodles, as in this heavenly dish.

SERVES 4

½ tsp cumin seeds

½ tsp coriander seeds

6 oz (168 g) tomoshiraga somen noodles

2 tsp (10 ml) vegetable oil

12 Chicken Meatballs (page 101), cooked

2 tbsp (30 ml) water

2 tbsp (30 ml) Spicy Plum Barbecue Sauce (page 167)

½ tsp black peppercorns, toasted and crushed

2 tbsp (2 g) finely chopped cilantro, for garnish

Toast the cumin and coriander seeds in a small pan over low heat until you smell the spices and the cumin is lightly brown, 1 minute. Turn off the heat and let cool. Crush the seeds in a mortar and pestle or use a grinder to powder it. Set aside.

Cook the noodles according to the manufacturer's instructions, drain and cool.

In a nonstick pan, add the oil and let it get lightly hot. Add the meatballs and toss around for 2 minutes until they get a good caramelized color. Then add the powdered spices, turn down the heat and keep stirring and tossing until the spices lose their raw flavor, 1 to 2 minutes. Add the water to cook the spices and turn the heat up to let the water evaporate. Add the barbecue sauce and simmer to blend the flavors.

Add the cooked noodles and toss very well. Sprinkle with the pepper and chopped cilantro.

Plum
Barbecue
Sauce

TOMATO-GARLIC CHICKEN NAAN PIZZA

Naan pizza has become a trend now, and why not? It is so simple to make and it turns a flatbread into a delicious meal in just a few minutes. You can use store-bought naan, but I love making my own. My recipe is yeast free and super quick. Add a basic chicken masala, onions, tomatoes and good fresh mozzarella, and this is faster than a phone call to your favorite pizza joint!

SERVES 4

10 cloves garlic

1 red onion, roughly diced

3 ripe tomatoes, quartered

¼ cup (60 ml) vegetable oil

1 lb (454 g) skinless, boneless chicken breasts, halved lengthwise and cut into ½" (1.3-cm) pieces

2 tbsp (16 g) chili powder or paprika

1 tsp garam masala

⅓ tsp turmeric

1 tsp ground coriander

½ tsp ground cumin

1 tbsp (18 g) salt

3 tbsp (45 ml) cream

⅓ cup (6 g) finely chopped cilantro

4 naan (page 25), or store-bought

TOPPINGS

1 lb (454 g) fresh mozzarella, sliced

10 cherry tomatoes, sliced horizontally

1 onion, thinly sliced

Red pepper flakes

A few Thai basil leaves, sliced

1 recipe Yogurt Sauce (page 164)

In a blender, combine the garlic, onion and tomatoes and blend to a smooth paste.

In a heavy-bottomed pan, add the oil and let it get hot. Turn the heat to a simmer and then add the tomato mixture to the oil; be careful, as the oil might splash. Add the chicken pieces, chili powder, garam masala, turmeric, coriander, cumin and salt. Turn the heat up to medium-high and let the mixture bubble up. Cover and cook for 20 minutes, or until the liquid is dry and the chicken is completely cooked. Uncover, add the cream and cilantro and mix well. This mixture should be thick and not runny at all. Turn off the heat and set aside until ready to use.

Preheat the oven to 500°F (250°C, or gas mark 10). Place a pizza or baking stone on the top rack of the oven. (You are just melting the cheese, so you could use the broiler too, but keep watch so you don't burn the cheese.)

To top the pizza, take a cooked naan, spoon a ladleful of the chicken mixture on top and then add some sliced mozzarella. Top it with some sliced tomatoes and onion and sprinkle with red pepper flakes. Place on the pizza stone and bake until the edges are brown and the mozzarella is melted. Remove from the oven and top with some basil. Drizzle with the yogurt sauce.

Notes: You can make the naan and chicken ahead of time. Just bake them when ready to eat.

This chicken can also be filled in wraps or served with rice.

PEPPERY CHICKEN LIVER STIR-FRY

There was this time I went into a small restaurant in India. I rarely go out to eat in India, and when I do I try to eat authentic spicy dishes and at places with character. I like dishes that have a story, dishes that came from grandma's kitchen. In fact, the name of the restaurant was along those lines, Old Grandma's Kitchen. It was run by a family who converted their 200-year-old home into a small eatery. On the green paint-chipped walls hung pictures of people with turbans and ladies with their beautiful *Kanchivaram* saris. They opened up for few hours in the afternoon and you could not reserve. They had enough food prepared and would not turn away anyone. The seating was basic simplicity and reminded me of my *aaya's* 100-year-old home. The owners came to each table, spoke about the dishes and explained anything we asked. And I did ask a lot of questions. I remember going back to them for some history lessons and was careful not to step over boundaries about their recipes.

Chicken liver prepared this way is very popular in South India. Curry leaf is one of the most important ingredients in this dish. There are few ingredients, but each one is very important.

SERVES 4–6

---

10 oz (280 g) chicken liver, washed and patted dry

1 tsp mildly hot chili powder or ground paprika

½ tsp ground coriander

½ tsp ground cumin

⅓ tsp garam masala

⅓ tsp turmeric

3 tbsp (45 ml) vegetable oil

⅓ cup (45 g) broken cashews

10 fresh curry leaves (don't skip this)

1 tbsp (10 g) freshly ground black pepper

⅓ cup (6 g) finely chopped cilantro

In a mixing bowl, combine the chicken liver, chili powder, coriander, cumin, garam masala and turmeric and mix well. Cover and marinate in the refrigerator for a minimum of 30 minutes or up to 2 hours.

In a shallow pan, preferably a *kadai* or a cast-iron pan, add the oil and let it get hot. Add the cashews and curry leaves and fry until the cashews turn slightly golden brown. Immediately remove them from the pan with a slotted spoon, place on a plate and set aside.

In the same pan, add the marinated liver and sauté for 5 minutes, tossing continuously. Cover and cook for 10 minutes over low heat. Uncover and add the pepper, toasted cashews-curry leaves and cilantro. Toss well.

Note: Serve this with some toasted wild rice or plain rice.

CORIANDER-SPICED PULLED CHICKEN WRAPS

When you make this dish, you might have your doubts. Trust me: wait until you sauté the vegetables and add the shredded chicken to it. You will be pleasantly surprised. The key is to keep the vegetables crunchy and sauté them with the chicken when you are ready to build the wrap. That way, it's hot and fresh. It's a simple technique to keep the chicken super moist and it soaks up all the spices while it boils in the spiced water. This dish is light and satisfying.

SERVES 4–6

CHICKEN

4 chicken breasts, washed and patted dry

3–4 cups (705–940 ml) water, as needed

⅓ tsp turmeric

1 tsp salt, divided

1½ tbsp (9 g) ground coriander

1½ tbsp (9 g) chili powder

1 tbsp (6 g) ground cumin

2 tbsp (30 ml) vegetable oil

1 large onion, finely chopped

3 tbsp (3 g) finely chopped cilantro

SLAW

2 tbsp (30 ml) vegetable oil

1 red bell pepper, cored, seeded and thinly sliced

1 green bell pepper, cored, seeded and thinly sliced

¼ red cabbage, thinly sliced

1 tsp sugar

Salt and pepper

⅓ cup (6 g) chopped cilantro

4–6 chapathis, tortillas, pita breads or burger buns

1 recipe Yogurt Sauce (page 164)

To make the chicken, in a saucepan, combine the chicken, 3 cups (705 ml) of the water, turmeric and ½ teaspoon of the salt, bring to a boil, lower the heat, cover and cook until the chicken is 80 percent cooked, or about 15 minutes. When you use a fork to tear the chicken, it should be easy, and it should not be pink in the center. Now you should have only about 1 cup (235 ml) water left in the pan. If not, add more water to make up the difference. Add the coriander, chili powder, cumin and remaining ½ teaspoon salt and let it simmer, uncovered, for about 10 minutes. Turn off the heat.

Remove the chicken from the pot, reserving the liquid in the pot, and place on a cleaning cutting board. With 2 forks, shred the chicken very well. Set aside.

Heat the oil in a sauté pan over medium heat, add the onion and fry until golden brown, about 2 minutes. Add the shredded chicken and ⅓ cup (80 ml) of the sauce from the pot and let it sizzle and dry up a bit. Add the chopped cilantro and turn off the heat. Set aside until you are ready to wrap it up.

To make the slaw, heat the oil in a sauté pan over medium heat. Add all the vegetables and sauté for 1 minute. Do not let it soften a lot, keeping the crunch. Add the sugar and salt and pepper to taste and let it sauté for 1 minute more. Turn off the heat, add the cilantro and stir to combine.

Warm the chapathis on a stove top griddle or toast the burger buns. Top with some shredded chicken, then the slaw and then a drizzle of yogurt sauce.

Note: This is traditionally wrapped in chapathis, a layered flatbread. You can find the flatbread in Indian grocery stores. If not, a warmed tortilla works perfectly.

CHICKEN SOUP WITH VEGETABLE-STUFFED WONTONS

Here's my take on chicken soup with dumplings. Chicken soup was not for sick days. In our home growing up, chicken soup was lunch on Sundays. We had rice, and we would liberally mix the soup with the rice and enjoy it. I love wontons (momos) stuffed with minced chicken, egg and different kinds of vegetables. Although I love to make my wrappers, which I find to be a very therapeutic process, store-bought wonton wrappers work perfectly well.

SERVES 4–6

WONTONS

½ red onion, finely chopped

½ cup (45 g) chopped red cabbage

½ cup (50 g) grated carrot

2 tbsp (2 g) finely chopped cilantro

2 scallions, thinly sliced

2 tsp (6 g) minced fresh ginger

2 tsp (10 g) minced garlic

2 green chiles, finely grated, or to taste

¼ tsp turmeric

¼ tsp ground cumin

1 tsp soy sauce

20 round wonton wrappers or fresh wrappers (see Note)

CHICKEN SOUP

1 tbsp (14 g) ghee

1 tbsp (10 g) lightly crushed pepper

½ tsp cumin seeds

4 cloves

½" (1.3-cm) cinnamon stick

1 tbsp (9 g) raw rice

½ red onion, finely diced

6 cloves garlic, chopped

1 lb (454 g) bone-in chicken pieces

⅓ tsp turmeric

1 tsp chili powder

1 tsp salt

4 cups (940 ml) chicken stock or water

½ cup (8 g) finely chopped cilantro, plus more for serving

To make the wontons, in a mixing bowl, combine all the ingredients except the wrappers and mix well. Place a wonton wrapper on your work surface, fill with 1 teaspoon of the filling, brush the sides with some water and pinch it together. Place on a plate dusted with flour and keep covered with a damp cloth. Repeat to fill all the wrappers. Set aside until you are ready to cook.

To make the soup, you can use a pressure cooker, an electric cooker, a slow cooker or a regular pot. In a pressure cooker, add the ghee and let it get hot. Add the pepper, cumin seeds, cloves, cinnamon stick and rice and fry for 30 seconds, until you smell the spices. Add the onion and garlic, turn the heat to medium-low and fry until golden brown, about 2 minutes. Don't let it burn. Add the chicken, turmeric, chili powder and salt. Toss well and brown the chicken for 2 minutes. Add the stock, bring to a boil and add the cilantro. Put on the lid and let it pressure cook for 4 to 5 whistle sounds. Turn off the heat and let the pressure go down for at least 15 minutes before opening it. If you are cooking in a pot, you have to let it simmer for about an hour for all the flavors of the soup to come together. Open the pot and drop the wontons into the soup; let boil for 5 minutes. Serve hot with fresh cilantro leaves.

Note: To make fresh wonton wrappers, mix 1 cup (96 g) of all-purpose flour, ½ teaspoon salt and ½ cup (120 ml) of water to make a hard dough. Knead very well and rest for 30 minutes to an hour. Then take half the size of a golf ball and roll it to thin sheets and stack them with some all-purpose flour in between so they don't stick to each other. Use it immediately.

CHICKEN CURRY SOUP WITH RICE CRACKERS

Here's my version of chicken tortilla soup, inspired by a popular dish called kori rotti from the region of Mangalore. Kori means "chicken" and rotti means "flatbread," but in this dish we use rice crackers. The color of the dish comes from the red chiles. Let the chicken sit and soak in the flavors for a couple of hours before serving.

SERVES 4–6

CURRY MASALA PASTE

2 tbsp (28 g) ghee, more as needed

5 small dried red chiles, or to taste

1 tbsp (6 g) coriander seeds

½ tsp peppercorns

¼ tsp fenugreek seeds (methi)

1 tsp cumin seeds

1" (2.5-cm) cinnamon stick

1 cardamom pod, slightly bruised

2 cloves

1 onion, sliced

8-9 cloves garlic, with skin on

½ cup (40 g) fresh or frozen grated coconut

⅛ tsp turmeric

½ lime-sized ball of tamarind or ½ tsp tamarind paste

1 whole chicken, 2–3 lb (908–1362 g), chopped into 2" (5-cm) pieces

Salt

1 cup (235 ml) thin coconut milk

FOR SERVING

1 tbsp (14 g) ghee

1 onion, thinly sliced

Chopped fresh cilantro

White or brown rice crackers

To make the curry masala paste, in a heavy-bottomed pan, heat the ghee and roast the red chiles, coriander seeds, peppercorns, fenugreek seeds, cumin seeds, cinnamon, cardamom and cloves over low heat for 2 minutes; do not let the spices burn. The spices will tell you when they are ready, about 2 minutes. Remove to a plate and let cool. Grind the toasted spices to a fine paste using a little water and reserve.

Next, fry the onion and garlic in the same pan, adding more ghee if needed, until golden brown, 2 minutes, then add the coconut and turmeric and sauté for 1 minute. After you see the coconut turn light brown, add the tamarind, bring to a boil, lower the heat and add the chicken, season with salt and toss and brown for 2 to 3 minutes, adding more ghee if necessary. Then add the ground spices, stir to combine and sauté until the pan is a little dry. Cover the pan and cook over medium heat until the chicken is tender, 25 to 30 minutes or until the chicken is tender.

When the chicken is cooked, add the coconut milk and bring to a boil for just a couple of seconds. Turn off the heat.

For serving, in a smaller pan, heat the ghee, add the sliced onion and fry until golden brown, 2 to 3 minutes. Add to the curry. Cover the pan immediately to trap the aroma. Sprinkle with cilantro and serve hot with crispy rice crackers to soak up the sauce.

Notes: Rice crackers can be found in an Indian or Asian grocery store. In an Indian grocery store, they are called vathal or fryums.

EGGPLANT ROLLATINI STUFFED WITH MINCED GARLICKY FISH

My aunt in Mysore is known for her sorra puttu, or fish mince. I ate it for years, enjoying and having no clue how it was made. The summer of 2002 when I visited India was when I learned how to make it. I remember the year so well because that was the first time I brought my two-year-old to visit family. My mum was so excited to introduce new and simple foods to him. I was absolutely astounded at how easy the dish was. "That's it?!" I remember asking. Now I stuff it in rolled eggplant slices. When I find wild-caught tilapia, that is the fish I use for this dish. Use any good white fish you find that day. Serve with some Coconut Rice with Peas (page 86) or herbed rice.

SERVES 4-6

---

1 large eggplant

2 tbsp (30 ml) olive oil

⅔ tsp salt, divided

⅛ tsp freshly group black pepper

2 halibut fillets (about 2 lb [908 g])

1 tsp canola oil

10 curry leaves, finely chopped

10 cloves garlic, thinly sliced

3 green chiles, finely diced

1 red onion, finely diced

½ tsp chili powder or mild paprika

⅛ tsp turmeric

⅛ tsp garam masala

⅛ cup (6 g) finely chopped cilantro

Preheat the oven to 350°F (180°C, or gas mark 4). Line a baking sheet with parchment paper.

Thinly slice the eggplant into long strips and lay them on the prepared baking sheet. Brush the eggplant with olive oil on both sides and sprinkle both sides with ⅓ teaspoon of the salt and the pepper. Bake for 10 minutes, or until softened. Remove from the oven and let cool.

Wash and pat dry the fish fillets. Place a flat-bottomed pan over medium heat and let it get hot. Add the canola oil, and once it gets hot, add the curry leaves and the garlic. Sauté for about 1 minute, or until the garlic is slightly cooked. Add the green chiles and onion and fry for 1 minute, then add the chili powder, turmeric and remaining ⅓ teaspoon salt; stir to combine.

Place the fish fillets on the onion mixture, cover with a lid, decrease the heat to low and cook for 7 minutes. Open the lid, add the garam masala and chopped cilantro and stir with a wooden spatula to break the fish apart into small bits. Let all the flavors mix and cook for another minute. Turn off the heat.

Have a serving dish ready. Carefully place an eggplant slice on your work surface, place 2 tablespoons (30 g) of the fish mixture along the edge and roll it gently; place in the serving dish. Repeat to use up the eggplant slices and fish mixture. Sprinkle with the fresh cilantro.

Notes: You can use any white mild-flavored fish you want. Sable fish or black cod works well, too. This dish is fully cooked, so it's just a serving suggestion to roll the eggplant. You can serve the fish mince with rice, too.

TANDOORI-SPICED FISH AND YUCA GARLIC CHIPS

I came up with this combo when I was watching a program on the Food Network about America and its comfort food. This is the Indian version and I proudly love it. The fish is marinated with spices that leave it moist and flaky, and the acidic touch finishes everything off with a sweet and spicy note. The yuca chips are unexpected and very satisfying. It's a spicy notch up from the regular fish and chips. This is the type of platter you should be ready to keep refilling.

SERVES 4–6

4 large pieces halibut (about 3 lb [1.3 kg])

MARINADE

1 tsp fresh garlic paste

1 tsp fresh ginger paste

½ tsp garam masala

1 tsp Kashmiri red chili powder, or to taste

1 tsp ground coriander

½ tsp ground cumin

1 tsp crushed dried fenugreek leaves (kasoori methi)

2 tbsp (16 g) chickpea flour

2 tsp thick yogurt

½ tsp lemon juice

1 tsp salt

2 tsp (10 ml) vegetable oil, plus more for frying

YUCA CHIPS

1 large yuca root

4 cloves garlic, finely chopped

2 tbsp (2 g) chopped fresh cilantro

Salt

Lemon wedges, for serving

Wash the fish and pat dry very well. Dice into 2-inch (5-cm) pieces and set aside.

To make the marinade, mix all the ingredients for the marinade in a bowl, add the fish cubes and gently turn to coat all sides. Cover and refrigerate for at least 1 hour or up to overnight.

Add 1 teaspoon of vegetable oil to a nonstick pan over medium heat and let it heat up. Fry the coated fish pieces. Turn after 1 minute on each side. This fish cooks fast, so keep an eye on it.

Transfer to paper towels to drain.

To make the yuca chips, peel and slice the yuca root thinly. Pat it dry. Pour the oil to a depth of 3 inches (7.5 cm) into a pot and heat to medium-high on a deep-frying thermometer. Fry the chips in batches until golden brown, about 2 minutes, and place on paper towels to drain. Sprinkle immediately with the garlic, cilantro and salt to taste. Serve with the fish and wedges of lemon for diners to squeeze over the fish.

Note: Because we don't deep-fry this fish, halibut works beautifully in this dish. You can alternatively use cod or king mackerel. Any white, fleshy fish will work.

Yuca root is quite hard to peel and cut, so I recommend using a very sharp knife. Cut it into halves, then peel and use a mandoline or slice it with a knife.

FISH TACOS

I was asked to create a recipe for a restaurant. Their requirement was that it should taste like an Indian-style fish taco. I remember the first evening when this dish was introduced to the customers: it sold, and it was made a regular on the menu. I am so proud of it. The curry sauce and the cilantro chutney work well together. You can use any fish you like, but try to find one with few bones.

SERVES 4–5

Vegetable oil, as needed

8–10 corn tortillas

Hot sauce (optional)

DRY RUB

½ tsp paprika

½ tsp dry mustard

1 tsp cayenne pepper

1 tsp ground cumin

1 tsp freshly groun black pepper

½ tsp white pepper

½ tsp dried thyme, crushed

1 tsp salt

2 (8-oz [227-g]) fillets flaky white fish

SLAW

1 cup (90 g) thinly sliced red cabbage

2 carrots, grated into long strips or thinly sliced

1 cup (90 g) broccoli slaw

Salt and pepper

SALSA

1 onion, finely diced

1 tomato, seeded and finely diced

1 jalapeño, finely chopped

Salt

Lime juice

FOR ASSEMBLY

1 recipe Apple Cilantro Chutney (page 162)

1 recipe Almond Curry Sauce (page 163)

Boursin cheese or cojita, for serving

Lime wedges

In a nonstick pan, add a teaspoon of oil, let it get hot and then crisp up the tortillas. You can add a few dashes of hot sauce on one side of the tortilla for the first layer of flavor. Shape them like a taco shell, and keep in between two glasses or bowls to hold the shape. You can put them in a low oven to crisp up more, if desired. Set aside.

To make the dry rub, combine all the ingredients in a bowl. Rub and pat the fish with a teaspoon of the mix on both sides. If you want it spicier, add more of the rub. Cover it and let it marinate in the refrigerator for 30 minutes.

Heat 2 to 3 tablespoons (30 to 45 ml) of vegetable oil in a nonstick pan over medium heat and carefully lay the fish in the pan. Cook for 2 to 3 minutes on each side, until the fish flakes easily with a fork. Remove from the heat and use a fork to flake the fish, or serve it as a fillet. Set aside.

To make the slaw, heat 1 teaspoon of oil in a pan over medium heat. Add the cabbage, carrot and broccoli to the pan, season with salt and pepper and lightly sauté for 1 minute. Transfer to a bowl and set aside.

To make the salsa, in a small bowl, combine the onion, tomato, jalapeño, salt and lime juice to taste and set aside.

(continued)

FISH TACOS (CONT.)

To assemble, place one tortilla on your work surface. Add some slaw, then some fish and salsa on top. Drizzle with the chutney and curry sauces and sprinkle with cheese. Serve immediately with lime wedges and hot sauce.

Notes: If you can't find cojita, a good feta cheese works well. You can stuff the tortillas and serve or keep all the components separately and have a party where everyone can choose what they want to add. Instead of the fish rub, you can use the taco seasoning below.

TACO SEASONING

MAKES A LITTLE LESS THAN 3 TABLESPOONS (18 G)

1 tbsp (8 g) chili powder

¼ tsp garlic powder

¼ tsp onion powder

¼ tsp red pepper flakes

¼ tsp dried oregano

½ tsp paprika

1½ tsp ground cumin

1 tsp sea salt

1 tsp black pepper

Mix all the ingredients in a small bowl. Store in an airtight container.

HARISSA ROAST CHICKEN WITH RICE AND EGGS

Roast chicken happens twice a year, once for the year-end holidays and once when I have a big party at home. I wonder why I don't make it more often. It's truly an impressive meal that doesn't take long to make. Smother, marinate, forget it and then bake. That's about it. I like to bake a whole chicken in a low oven and crank the heat up when it's almost ready to be taken out to crisp the skin. I also find that baking the chicken in a cast-iron pan helps with a good crust. Harissa has a lot of common ingredients to a tomato pickle that we make in India. Make the harissa in advance and it can be stored for a long time and used in many dishes. Serve with herbed rice or Coconut Rice with Peas (page 86).

SERVES 4

⅓ cup (80 g) Harissa (page 165)

2 tsp (8 g) ginger garlic paste

1 tsp dark brown sugar

4 tsp (20 ml) vegetable oil

Salt and pepper

½ cup (112 g) unsalted butter, at room temperature

1 (5-lb [2.3-kg]) whole kosher chicken (organic chicken if only that is available)

⅓ cup (6 g) finely chopped cilantro, for garnish

Lemon, for serving

4 hard-boiled eggs, quartered

In a mixing bowl, combine the harissa, ginger garlic paste, dark brown sugar and oil. Mix well. Check for salt. The harissa has salt, but you want to add another ½ to 1 teaspoon of salt for the chicken.

Add 2 tablespoons (30 g) of the harissa mixture to the softened unsalted butter and mix well; rub the mixture in between the skin and the flesh of the chicken and spread evenly. Cover the chicken with the remaining paste and tie the legs together. Let it marinate for 2 hours or overnight. I leave mine overnight in the refrigerator.

Preheat the oven to 425°F (220°C, or gas mark 7). Place the rack in the middle of the oven.

Place the chicken in a cast-iron skillet, put it in the oven and turn the oven temperature down to 350°F (180°C, or gas mark 4). Bake the bird for 1 hour and 30 minutes. Every 20 minutes, baste the chicken with the juices and oil that have dripped into the pan. If you find the top browning too much, put a tent on it with an aluminum foil. That will make the chicken very moist. Once the chicken is cooked and the juices run clear when you slice a little bit from the side, take it out of the oven and let it rest for at least 10 minutes before carving it. Carefully carve the pieces and place on a serving dish.

Top with cilantro and serve with lemon wedges for squeezing over. Drizzle with some drippings to keep it moist. Serve with the hard-boiled eggs.

*See photo on page 90.

NUT-CRUSTED HALIBUT WITH GREEN ONION SAUCE

The second year of our marriage, when I grew a little comfortable with cooking and a little relaxed around my kitchen, I planned to make something out of my comfort zone, something completely different. I made this effortlessly chic dish for Valentine's Day. I recall how impressed my hubby was, and how happy I was. I told myself, "Oh hey, I can cook." I scribbled in my diary so that I didn't forget anything, thinking that I would put this recipe in my cookbook, whenever that happens—and here it is. It's a surreal feeling that this recipe made it. If there's one thing you do not want to skip is the asafetida. Get a small bottle; it keeps for a while. Serve the fish with some chunky, toasted bread or herbed rice.

SERVES 2

FISH

2 (8-oz [27-g]) halibut fillets

¼ cup (35 g) toasted hazelnuts, crushed

¼ cup (30 g) fine semolina

½ tsp red chili powder

⅓ tsp turmeric

1 tsp lemon zest

½ tsp salt

2 large eggs

2 tbsp (30 ml) cream or milk

Pinch of salt

¼ cup (60 ml) vegetable oil, divided

GREEN ONION SAUCE

1 tsp vegetable oil

4 scallions, sliced

⅓ tsp asafetida

⅓ tsp turmeric

¼ cup (60 ml) thick coconut milk

⅓ tsp salt

⅓ tsp freshly ground black pepper

Preheat the oven to 350°F (180°C, or gas mark 4). Line a baking sheet with parchment paper.

To make the fish, wash and pat dry the halibut fillets. Take 2 plates. On one plate, add the crushed hazelnuts, semolina, red chili powder, turmeric, lemon zest and salt. Mix well and set aside. On another shallow plate, break the eggs and beat in the cream and salt with a fork.

Place a nonstick griddle over medium-high heat. Add 2 tablespoons (30 ml) of the oil and let it get hot. Take 1 fish fillet, dip it in the egg-cream mixture fully and then add it to the nut mixture. Pat the mixture very well onto both sides and then carefully slide it into the pan. Turn the heat to medium-low and cook the fish about 3 minutes on each side, until tender and flaky. Transfer to the prepared baking sheet. Repeat with the second fish fillet and the remaining 2 tablespoons (30 ml) of oil.

Place the baking sheet in the oven and bake for 5 minutes, or until the fish is cooked through and flakes easily with a fork.

To make the sauce, add the oil to a saucepan over medium heat and let it get hot. Add the scallion and asafetida and slightly sweat for about a minute. Then add the turmeric and coconut milk. Simmer for 2 minutes and then add the salt and pepper.

Place the fish on 2 plates. Pour the sauce over the fish and serve.

Notes: You can use any fleshy fish that does not have a strong smell. You can finish cooking the fish in the pan by covering and cooking over very low heat for a few minutes. It will not be as crispy because it will steam when you cover, but it is an option.

CURRIED SHRIMP SKEWERS WITH PINEAPPLE

It would be wise to double this recipe. The curry powder adds a nice color and not too much heat. The moment the marinated shrimp hit the hot cast-iron pan, the sizzle and the first blister it creates is magical. It takes minutes for the tail to touch the head; when that happens, remove the shrimp from the pan and finish it off with a squeeze of lime juice.

SERVES 4–6

1½ lb (680 g) raw shrimp (I used U10, but any size is fine), peeled and deveined

4 cloves garlic, minced

1 tbsp (6 g) curry powder

½ tsp freshly ground black pepper

1 tbsp (15 ml) coconut milk

½ tsp dark brown sugar

¼ tsp kosher salt, or more to taste

½ tsp lime zest

Juice of 1 lime, or to taste

½ fresh pineapple, cut into bite-sized chunks

1 green bell pepper, cored, seeded and cut into 1" (2.5-cm) squares

2–3 tbsp (30–45 ml) vegetable oil

Lime wedges, for serving

Chopped chives, for garnish

Wash and pat dry the shrimp very well.

In a mixing bowl, combine the minced garlic, curry powder, black pepper, coconut milk, dark brown sugar, salt, lime zest and lime juice. Mix well. Add the shrimp, turn to coat and marinate for 20 minutes; do not go over 20 minutes because the shrimp will start cooking in the acidity of the lime juice and you don't want that.

You can skewer the shrimp on a metal skewer or a bamboo skewer soaked in water for an hour. Skewer 3 to 4 shrimp, alternating with the pineapple and bell pepper.

Preheat a cast-iron flat-bottomed skillet over medium-high heat. Once hot, add some of the oil and gently add a skewer to cook. Do not crowd the pan. Add a few at a time, adding more oil and letting it get hot between batches. Once you see the shrimp turn get pink, about 1 minute, turn it and cook on the other side. Once the tail touches the head, it's done. Remove to a serving plate.

Serve immediately with lime wedges and add chives for garnish.

Notes: You can stuff the shrimp in tortillas or serve them over rice for a full meal. This is perfect for a cocktail party, too.

For an extra layer of flavor, you can coat the shrimp in chickpea flour or bread crumbs and then panfry.

CURRIED CRAB CORN CHOWDER

If you are in a luxurious mood and can find fresh crabmeat, make this chowder. It is a rich and delicious dish. I'm all for using frozen corn and peas, but do not skimp on good crabmeat. Add a splash of wine if you are really in the mood. The chowder thickens as it sits, so you can add an extra cup (235 ml) of stock if you want it soupier.

SERVES 4–6

1 tbsp (15 ml) vegetable or extra virgin olive oil

2 tbsp (28 g) unsalted butter

1 fresh bay leaf

2 stalks celery, very finely chopped

1 red onion, very finely chopped

3 cloves garlic, grated or minced

½ tsp salt, divided

2 russet potatoes, peeled and diced into small cubes

Freshly ground black pepper

1 tbsp (6 g) madras curry powder

½ tsp Old Bay Seasoning (optional)

2 tbsp (16 g) all-purpose flour

2 cups (470 ml) vegetable or chicken stock

2 cups (470 ml) light coconut milk, canned or fresh

1 cup (235 ml) milk

3 cups (450 g) fresh or frozen corn kernels

8 oz (224 g) cooked lump crabmeat or fresh

⅓ tsp roasted fennel powder

3–4 chives, finely snipped, for garnish

2 tsp (1 g) chopped fresh cilantro

Heat a large pot over medium heat and add the oil and butter. Let the butter melt, then add the bay leaf. Let the bay leaf sizzle and ooze some flavor into the butter. Then add the celery and onion and cook, stirring continuously, for a couple of minutes, then add the garlic and ¼ teaspoon of the salt and sauté for 2 minutes.

Add the potatoes and sauté for a minute. Then add the pepper, curry powder and Old Bay and cook over medium heat to take some of the rawness out of the curry powder. After it cooks for about 1 minute, add the flour, and cook, stirring, for 2 to 3 minutes. Add the broth and use a whisk to thoroughly combine everything. Add the coconut milk and milk. Keep stirring and bring to a boil, then reduce the heat to medium, add the corn and crabmeat and simmer for 5 minutes. Adjust the seasonings and add the fennel powder and the remaining ¼ teaspoon salt if needed. Remove the bay leaf. Serve, garnishing each bowl with the chopped chives and cilantro.

PO' BOY WITH FRIED SHRIMP

This sandwich can literally be put together in 30 minutes. I know—I've timed myself. This is my take on the true American sandwich. I have sampled so many versions of the po' boy and the one I've enjoyed the most is the sandwich that is dipped in a sauce just before serving. Thanks go to the state of Louisiana for giving this sandwich to us. In no way is this traditional, just an inspired sandwich. I was told by a very famous chef, DO NOT skimp on the mayo and you have to have a good, crusty French bread.

SERVES 4

12–15 raw tiger shrimp, cleaned and deveined

2 tsp salt, plus more to taste

1 tsp ginger garlic paste

½ tsp Kashmiri red chili powder

⅓ tsp turmeric

1 tbsp (15 ml) fresh lemon juice

CRISPY COATING

2 tsp rice flour

⅓ cup (40 g) fine semolina

⅓ tsp red chili powder

Pinch of salt

MANGO COMPOTE

1 tsp oil

1 tsp toasted cumin, lightly crushed

½ red onion, finely chopped

1 serrano pepper

⅓ tsp turmeric

½ tsp salt

2 ripe Alphonso mangoes, peeled, seeded and finely diced

2 tbsp (28 g) mayonnaise

Vegetable oil, for shallow frying

1 loaf crusty French bread, cut into 6″ (15-cm) lengths

Sliced tomato, lightly salted

Lettuce

Pat dry the tiger shrimp and place in a bowl. Add the salt and massage it into the shrimp well; let it sit for 10 minutes. This will make the shrimp juicy and plump. After 10 minutes, rinse the shrimp under cold water and again pat dry completely.

In a bowl, combine the ginger garlic paste, Kashmiri red chili powder, turmeric, lemon juice and a pinch of salt; add the shrimp, mix well and let marinate for 10 to 15 minutes.

Meanwhile, to make the coating, combine all the ingredients on a shallow plate.

To make the mango compote, heat the oil in a pan over medium heat. Add the cumin seeds and sauté for 1 minute, until you smell the spice. Add the onion and sauté until it is browned a bit, 2 minutes. Add the serrano pepper, turmeric and salt and sauté for 1 minute. Set aside.

Add the mango flesh and mayonnaise to a blender and puree. Add the onion mixture to the pureed mango and mayo and check for seasoning. Chill in the refrigerator until ready to serve.

Place a large skillet over medium heat and add 2 to 3 tablespoons (30 to 45 ml) oil for frying the shrimp. Add the shrimp to the coating and coat generously, pressing the coating onto the shrimp to make sure it sticks. When the oil is hot, add a few shrimp at a time and cook until the outside is crispy, about 1½ minutes on each side. Do not crowd the pan. Remove to drain on paper towels and repeat to fry all the shrimp.

Spread some mango compote on the bottom of each piece of bread, add a few shrimp and top with tomato, lettuce and top piece of bread. Serve immediately.

CHAPTER 5

SWEET TREATS

Dessert first. Always.

If dessert were a religion, I would be its most pious follower. Feed me dessert before dinner, and I'll be your best friend forever. Have me over for a dessert party, and I might never leave. Yes, I do love my sugar and spice, but sugar more. I love vintage desserts, simple rustic desserts from the past, easy no-fuss desserts. I just love desserts.

One of my first professional baking lessons was from Le Cordon Bleu, in Paris. It was an overwhelming and exciting feeling to learn the art of the pretty macarons, the perfect meringue and the classic French éclair from some of the top pastry chefs there. I came back a bit taller, knowing that I could bake macarons. I proceeded to bake them for probably the next six months. They were daintily wrapped and given to teachers, at birthday parties and to friends, and I just kept making them because I would get so freakishly excited to see the smooth outer cover and tiny feet grow.

Still, there's always a part of me that loves the old things that I grew up with. The comfort zone is one hell of an addictive feeling. I created recipes just imagining some of the flavors I took a bite of when I was ten. Like the Honey Cake (page 150), for instance. It's a very Indian-flavored cake with cardamom, syrup and a lovely sponge that creates magic with your senses. The Coconut-Jaggery Bread Pudding (page 139) brings back memories of sweet, delicious evening meals. There is a variety of deep-fried goodness here, such as Apple-Cardamom Funnel Cake (page 135) and Banana Beignets (page 147), classic American treats with an Indian vibe. If you love your coffee like I do, then there's No-Churn Coffee Ice Cream (page 157). There's also the classic lassi in frozen pop form (page 158) to entertain kids big and small, and the Coconut, Dried Fruit and Nut Tart (page 149) that you probably will not want to share with anyone else.

This chapter is very close to my heart, with recipes that have been inspired by my mum to recipes I created especially for this book and for you. This chapter will delight your sweet tooth. I promise.

JAM BUNS

We walked thirty minutes in the evening on weekends. Every Saturday, mom and I would walk hand in hand, talk and chat. We were headed to the popular Iyengar Bakery on the corner of Commercial Street. We would stand in line to order our hot jam buns. When our turn came, my mom would order two to eat right away and a few to be wrapped for my dad. When we got our order, which was always still warm to the touch, we would walk a few steps away from the crowd, find a calm place and open up the box. Staring at us would be two beautiful buns, lightly warm, crisp on the outside, with just enough sugar for crunch, filled with red, gooey jam. Even now it makes me close my eyes and swoon. Now, the next best thing is to make my own. In my opinion, this jam bun, which is a little denser than a doughnut, is all about the warm jam. Be sure to warm up the jam just before filling and serve them right away.

MAKES 12 BUNS

2¼ tsp (1 packet, or 9 g) active dry yeast

1 tsp plus ¼ cup (50 g) plus ⅓ cup (65 g) sugar, divided

1 cup (235 ml) milk, warmed to 110°F (43°C)

4 cups (480 g) all-purpose flour, plus more for rolling and sprinkling

¼ tsp salt

1 tbsp (15 ml) vanilla extract

4 tbsp (56 g) unsalted butter, softened

2 eggs

Vegetable oil, for deep-frying

⅓ cup (80 g) Mixed Fruit Cardamom Jam (page 166)

In a small bowl, sprinkle the yeast and the 1 teaspoon sugar over the warm milk, stir and set aside to bubble up and activate.

In a standing mixer fitted with the paddle attachment, combine the flour, ¼ cup (50 g) of the sugar, salt and vanilla. Add the yeast mixture, butter and eggs and knead on medium speed for about 5 minutes, or until the dough comes together.

Turn out the dough onto a floured surface and roll to about ½ inch (1.3 cm) thick. Cut out rounds using a 3-inch (7.5-cm) biscuit cutter and place them a few inches (cm) apart on a lightly floured baking sheet. Sprinkle a little flour on top, cover with a lint-free kitchen towel and place them somewhere warm to rise for about 1½ hours, or until doubled in size.

Pour the vegetable oil to a depth of 4 inches (10 cm) into a heavy-duty pan and heat to 350°F (180°C) on a deep-frying thermometer. Pour the remaining ⅓ cup (65 g) sugar onto a shallow plate. Carefully lift the buns off the baking sheet and fry in batches until golden brown on both sides, about 2 minutes on each side. Remove with a spider and drain on paper towels. Dredge them in the sugar, dusting off the extra. Return the oil to temperature between batches and do not crowd the pan.

Warm the jam in a small pot or in the microwave and transfer to a cloth piping bag with a nozzle. Make a hole in the bun (not too deep) with the nozzle or a small knife. Place the nozzle in the hole and fill each bun with 1 tablespoon (14 g) of jam. Serve warm.

RICE PUDDING WITH ROASTED BLUEBERRIES AND PISTACHIOS

While I do like a chilled pudding with lots of pistachios, every once and a while I like it hot and steaming with butter drizzled over fresh berries. You can use a combination of milk and full cream, or just milk. Traditionally, full fat milk is used and it's just so creamy. The sweet, creamy texture, with a bite from the rice, goes very well with the floral scents of orange and blueberries.

SERVES 6—8

1 cup (210 g) short grain white rice

3 cups (710 ml) water

2 cups (475 ml) full fat milk

Pinch of salt

⅓ cup (65 g) white granulated sugar

1 star anise

5 whole green cardamom, lightly crushed

Pinch of saffron or 15 strands

2 tbsp (30 g) unsalted butter

⅓ cup (40 g) pistachios, slivered

⅓ cup (35 g) blueberries

1 tbsp (15 g) sugar

1 tbsp (10 g) orange zest

Wash the rice a couple of times and soak for 30 minutes.

Rinse the rice and in a thick-bottomed pot, add the water and bring to a boil. Lower to a simmer, cover and cook for 20 minutes.

Then add the milk, salt and sugar and mix well. Take a cheesecloth, for a bouquet garni, and add the star anise and green cardamom. Tie it tightly and drop it in the pot. Keep stirring every few minutes and let the rice cook in the milk. Cook this for another 15 to 20 minutes. It will be creamy and thick. Be cautious not to scorch the bottom. Turn off the heat.

Now, make brown butter by melting the unsalted butter in a thick-bottomed pan on low heat. It will melt and foam up, which will take about 5 minutes. Simmer it and the milk solids will brown and settle to the bottom. Once that happens, take it off the stove, cool and strain.

Next, add the brown butter to a sauté pan and let it get hot. Add the pistachios and toast it a bit. Add the blueberries and sugar and let the berries sweat out a bit and get soft, about 1 minute. Turn off the heat then add the zest. Drizzle this over the pudding and serve hot or cold.

APPLE-CARDAMOM FUNNEL CAKE

My weakness is fried food, and sweet fried food in particular. I wish I could tell you how much I crave sweet fried dough. I almost want to stop writing this and go downstairs to whip up the batter and make a batch, and it's 9:30 p.m.! These sugary, squiggly, funky-looking fried funnel cakes are drenched with confectioners' sugar and are insanely addictive. They don't soak up huge amounts of oil, so they are soft on the inside and crispy on the outside.

MAKES 10–12

Vegetable oil, for deep-frying

3 eggs

¼ cup (50 g) granulated sugar

2 cups (470 ml) whole milk

3½ cups (420 g) all-purpose flour

½ tsp baking powder

⅓ tsp baking soda

¼ tsp salt

⅓ tsp ground cardamom

1 Granny Smith apple, peeled and finely grated

Confectioners' sugar or ice cream, for serving

Pour the vegetable oil to a depth of 3 inches (7.5 cm) into a heavy-bottomed skillet and heat to 375°F (190°C) on a deep-frying thermometer.

In a large bowl, beat the eggs and granulated sugar together until smooth. Carefully beat in the milk. Add the flour, baking powder, baking soda and salt and beat until the batter smooth with no lumps. Add the cardamom and grated apple and fold in until combined.

Place half of the mixture into a gallon-sized (4-L) zip-top bag. Snip one of the bottom corners off and carefully let some batter pour into the hot oil. Make a large circle of the batter and connect it with more batter around and around in the pan. Let fry until golden brown on the first side, about 3 minutes. With tongs, turn the funnel cake over and let it brown on the second side for about 2 additional minutes.

Remove the funnel cake with a spider spoon and drain on paper towels. Repeat with more batter, bringing the oil back to temperature between batches. Sprinkle with confectioners' sugar. Serve hot.

FENNEL-SPICED CASHEW COOKIES

There's a level of sentimentality to these cookies. I enjoy nut-based desserts, and these cookies are undeniably good. The cardamom and fennel powder add just a bit of surprise and the pepper makes a spicy addition. It's a cookie that will scream of India when you take a bite.

MAKES 12

1½ cups (180 g) all-purpose flour, plus more for rolling

¼ cup (30 g) cashew powder

½ tsp baking powder

⅓ tsp salt

1½ sticks (12 tbsp [168 g]) unsalted butter, at room temperature

½ cup (60 g) confectioners' sugar

½ tsp green ground cardamom

½ tsp fennel seeds, toasted and powdered

6 black peppercorn, toasted and powdered

Pinch of saffron, crushed

2 tsp milk

½ tsp vanilla extract

2 tbsp (30 ml) rose water

½ cup (75 g) pistachios, finely chopped

Preheat the oven to 350°F (180°C, or gas mark 4). Line a baking sheet with parchment paper.

Sift the flour, cashew powder, baking powder and salt into a large bowl.

In a separate bowl, combine the butter and confectioners' sugar and beat with a mixer or whisk until light and fluffy. Add the flour mixture, cardamom, fennel, pepper and saffron and beat to combine. Add the milk, vanilla extract and rose water, 1 tablespoon (15 ml) at a time. The dough should be very thick. Mix until it comes together, but do not overwork the dough. Wrap the dough with a plastic wrap and chill for 20 minutes.

Sprinkle some flour onto the countertop and a rolling pin. Roll out the cookie dough to about ¼ inch (6 mm) thick. Sprinkle with some of the chopped pistachios. Using a cookie cutter, cut out shapes and transfer with a palette knife to the prepared baking sheet.

Turn the oven down to 325°F (170°C, or gas mark 3) and bake for 17 to 18 minutes, or until golden brown. Carefully transfer to a cooling rack and let cool completely before storing them in a cookie jar.

COCONUT-JAGGERY BREAD PUDDING

Mom would make this jaggery kheer, or sweet coconut stew, with chapathis at least once a week for dinner. It's like we had dessert for dinner! With dad and his sweet tooth, it was a special meal. Now, I make this as a treat. It goes so well as a dessert for parties or as part of a brunch table. Here I've used saffron bread, which I love, but you can use any rich bread you want.

SERVES 8–10

2 tbsp (28 g) unsalted butter, softened

16 slices Saffron Milk Bread (page 14), or any white bread

1 cup (80 g) grated fresh or frozen coconut

2 tbsp (22 g) poppy seeds, soaked in warm water to cover for 30 minutes and drained

4 cardamom pods

¾ cup (180 ml) water, divided

⅓ cup (65 g) crushed jaggery (you can substitute brown sugar, but the end result will not be authentic)

1 cup (235 ml) milk

10–15 raisins

3 tbsp (21 g) sliced almonds

Preheat the oven to 300°F (150°C, or gas mark 2).

Spread ¼ teaspoon of butter on each slice of bread. Line them up on a baking sheet and bake for 15 minutes, or until crispy and golden brown. Alternatively, you can toast and brown them on a griddle over low heat. Set aside and let cool.

In a blender, combine the grated coconut, poppy seeds, cardamom pods and ½ cup (120 ml) of the water and grind to a very smooth paste.

In a saucepan, combine the crushed jaggery and remaining ¼ cup (60 ml) water and let it simmer and melt over low heat. Once it is completely melted, don't stir. Let the dirt settle to the bottom and slowly pour off only the top part into another bowl, carefully leaving the dirt and grit on the bottom of the pan; discard.

In a clean saucepan, combine the drained jaggery and coconut paste and let it come to a boil over medium heat. Reduce the heat and let simmer for 5 minutes. Add the milk and simmer for 5 minutes longer. Turn off the heat. The mixture should be like a thick pancake batter. Let it cool.

Preheat the oven to 400°F (200°C, or gas mark 6) for 10 minutes. Lightly butter the bottom of an ovenproof dish.

Pour the cooked coconut mixture into the prepared dish. Arrange the toasted bread on top. Decorate with the raisins and almonds. Bake for 15 minutes, or until the top is brown and toasted, and serve immediately.

SESAME BRITTLE WITH ROSE WATER

It's hard to resist a good brittle. I've had this love-hate relationship with candy making, but once I found an incredibly easy method, I've never had to look at a candy thermometer again. The trick is to stir continuously and be patient while the sugar dissolves and it comes together in minutes.

MAKES ABOUT 2 DOZEN 2" (5-CM) PIECES

---

1 cup (150 g) white sesame seeds

½ cup (73 g) raw peanuts

½ cup (73 g) raw cashews

2-3 tbsp (28-42 g) ghee or browned butter, plus more for the cutting board

¾ cup (150 g) sugar

¼ cup grated jaggery or panela

5 green cardamom pods, powdered

1 tsp rose water or rose essence

Dry roast the sesame seeds in a large nonstick pan over medium heat for 2 to 3 minutes. Let the seeds plump a bit but do not let them turn brown. Transfer to a plate and let cool. In the same pan, toast the peanuts and cashews very lightly, or until the raw flavor is gone. Coarsely crush the nuts in a food processor or finely chop by hand. Set aside.

Grease a wooden cutting board thoroughly with ghee.

Melt the 2 to 3 tablespoons (28 to 42 g) ghee in a heavy-bottomed pan over medium heat. Add the sugar and jaggery and let it melt completely, stirring constantly, about 10 minutes. Once the sugar and jaggery is completely melted, add the toasted sesame seeds, nuts, ground cardamom and rose water. Keep mixing until everything comes together to form a ball, 2 to 3 minutes. Immediately transfer to the prepared board.

With the help of a flat plate, flatten it out a bit. It will be hot, so be careful. Then use a rolling pin and roll it out to ⅓-inch (8-mm) thick. Cut into shapes while it is hot and let cool on the board. Once it is completely cooled, transfer to an airtight container. It will keep for up to 2 months.

NO-BAKE PUMPKIN HALWA PIE

The first American dessert I fell in love with was pumpkin pie. I would go to Denny's after dinner just for a big slice of pumpkin pie with a huge dollop of whipped cream. Over the years, I've made many kinds of pumpkin pie and have not met one I didn't like. This version is a true mix of Indian and American. The filling is a halwa, which can be eaten as is or poured into a nutty crust. It is as straightforward as a dessert can get. Add any spice mix you want, such as ground cloves or cinnamon or even a mix. Be sure to let it set in the refrigerator before slicing. Serve topped with fruit and whipped cream.

SERVES 8 (MAKES A 7" OR 18-CM PIE)

CRUST

½ cup (73 g) raw almonds

½ cup (73 g) pistachios

15 dates, pitted

7 dried figs, chopped

2 tbsp (28 g) unsalted butter, melted

Pinch of salt

FILLING

1 (16-oz [454-g]) can plain pumpkin puree

½ cup (60 g) milk powder

1 cup (235 ml) full-fat milk, divided

3 tbsp (24 g) cornstarch

1 cup (200 g) fine sugar

½ cup (112 g) unsalted butter, melted and browned a bit (clarified butter)

½ tsp ground cardamom

½ tsp ground ginger

Pinch of saffron, crushed and soaked in 2 tsp (10 ml) milk

To make the crust, place all the ingredients in a food processor. Pulse until chopped to a chunky, sticky mixture. (Add a couple of tablespoons [15 to 30 ml] of cold water if needed.) Pat the dough into a 7-inch (18-cm) springform pan (or use a cake pan covered with plastic wrap). Flatten the dough out with your fingers or the back of a spoon. Chill in the refrigerator for 30 minutes.

To make the filling, in a heavy-bottomed pan, combine the pumpkin puree, milk powder and ¾ cup (180 ml) of the milk. Mix well and cook over medium-low heat until the mixture comes to a very thick consistency, about 15 minutes. Do not let the bottom burn, so keep stirring.

In a small cup, combine the remaining ¼ cup (60 ml) milk with the cornstarch and stir until smooth. Add the cornstarch mixture and the sugar to the pan and cook, stirring, over low heat for about 10 minutes, or until it is thick again. Add the clarified butter and cook, stirring, until the mixture leaves the sides of the pan, another 10 minutes. Add the cardamom, ginger and saffron with the milk. Turn off the heat and let the mixture cool. Stir so it doesn't form a film on top.

Pour into the cooled pie crust and chill for 30 minutes or overnight.

BOTTLE GOURD HALWA HAND PIES

This is a delicious labor of love. The bottle gourd halwa and the pie crust can be made ahead and stored separately. If you have a mold, it makes a cute package, but don't fret if you don't have one. Simply roll out the dough, cut into circles, fill a tablespoon of the filling, bring one side over and crimp with a fork. It's as easy as that.

MAKES 8 HAND PIES

FILLING

1 bottle gourd (lauki)

4 tbsp (56 g) ghee or unsalted butter, melted and browned, divided

½ cup (100 g) sugar

½ cup (60 g) full-fat or nonfat milk powder

3 tbsp (27 g) cashews

2 tbsp (18 g) raisins

2 tbsp (18 g) currants (optional)

CRUST

1¼ cups (150 g) whole wheat flour

¼ tsp plus ⅛ tsp fine salt, divided

½ cup (112 g) unsalted butter

2–3 tbsp (30–45 ml) cold water

FOR FINISHING

1 egg, beaten (for egg wash)

1 tbsp (12 g) sugar

To make the filling, peel the bottle gourd and cut in half lengthwise. Scoop out the seeds with a spoon. Finely grate the flesh with a hand grater or in a food processor. Place in a strainer and lightly squeeze the juice out of it. Discard the juice or use it for something else. Set aside the grated bottle gourd.

Heat a heavy-bottomed skillet over medium heat. Add 3 tablespoons (42 g) ghee and the grated bottle gourd and cook, stirring continuously so that the bottom doesn't scorch, for 15 to 20 minutes, until the vegetable is soft but still holds its shape. Add the sugar and milk powder and cook, stirring, until thickened and there is no liquid left, 3 to 4 minutes. Remove from the heat and let cool it completely.

Heat the remaining 1 tablespoon (14 g) ghee in a small pan and toast the cashews, raisins and currants (if using) over medium-low heat, being careful not to burn. Once the cashews are golden brown, add the mixture to the prepared filling and let cool completely before you make the pies.

To make the crust, whisk together the flour and salt in a large bowl and then cut in the butter with a pastry cutter or a fork until it looks like coarse meal. Add the water 1 tablespoon (15 ml) at a time, working the dough together with your fingertips just until it comes together, and adding only enough water so the dough comes together when you squeeze it. Gather the dough together into a ball and then flatted it into a disk; wrap it in plastic wrap and refrigerate until chilled, about 30 minutes.

(continued)

BOTTLE GOURD HALWA HAND PIES (CONT.)

Preheat the oven to 375°F (190°C, or gas mark 5). Remove the chilled dough from the refrigerator. Lay a piece of parchment paper out on your work surface, place the dough on it and top with another piece of parchment. Working from the center out, roll out the dough and use a 4-inch (10-cm) cookie cutter (or a glass with that diameter) to cut out 8 circles of dough. You may need to gather the scraps and reroll to get 8 circles. Roll each circle out to 5-inch (13-cm) circles, place 2 tablespoons (30 g) of the filling on one side, fold the circle in half over the filling and crimp the sides with a fork or just pinch it. Pierce a hole in the top and transfer to a baking tray. Chill for 20 to 30 minutes.

To finish the pies, brush the top with the egg wash and sprinkle with some sugar for a glossy, crispy, sugary top. Bake for 25 to 30 minutes, until golden. Let cool for 15 minutes before serving.

BANANA BEIGNETS

The car took us to a gated community. This was the first time I met her—my mom's Malayalee friend. I immediately took a liking to this aunty and her daughter, who was little younger than me. Aunt brought out a plate of what looked like fritters. She said they were ethakappam (pazham puri, or fried banana), but I was not a fan of how that sounded. I very sweetly said I wasn't hungry and ate the chips she gave me instead. I saw my mum and aunt have their tea and talk while I chatted with the little girl. It was time to leave and aunty packed me some fried banana because I hadn't eaten or tried it. On our way back home in the car, I got hungry. I opened up the box and took a bite of the banana fritter. I was pleasantly surprised, and it was addictive, too. To this day, I remember that fritter and how I fell in love with *Keralite* food. This is an ode to all my mom's friends. I've had the pleasure of eating some of the best *Kerala* dishes, and this is one of them.

MAKES 16 BEIGNETS

2 ripe bananas

½ cup (60 g) all-purpose flour

1 tbsp (8 g) rice flour

1–2 tbsp (12–24 g) sugar, as needed

⅓ tsp turmeric

⅓ tsp salt

¾–1 cup (180–235 ml) water, at room temperature

Vegetable oil, for deep-frying

Peel and slice the bananas into 4 equal pieces and then stand each piece up on the cutting board and cut in half vertically to make 8 slices total from each banana.

In a large bowl, combine the flours, sugar, turmeric and salt; stir to combine and then add the water and stir again. The batter should be thicker than pancake or idli batter.

Pour the oil to a depth of 3 to 4 inches (7.5 to 10 cm) into a deep pot and heat to 350°F (180°C) on a deep-frying thermometer. Dip the sliced bananas into the batter, slip into the oil and fry in batches until golden brown, 2 minutes. Remove from the oil with a spider and drain on paper towels. Return the oil to temperature between batches. Serve hot.

Notes: The bananas should be ripe but not overly ripe.

I normally use all-purpose flour (maida) for making the batter. You can also make these with half each all-purpose flour and whole wheat flour, or with only whole wheat flour.

You can dust the beignets with some confectioners' sugar for extra sweetness.

COCONUT, DRIED FRUIT AND NUT TART

When I was growing up, this was called coconut naan. It doesn't look like naan and it's not just coconut. This is my take on gujjia, a very popular Indian dessert made during festivals and a classic, vintage treat that we used to get in bakeries in India. The stuffing is what makes this dessert. Here I've combined coconut with dried fruits, which makes it perfect for celebrations. I have used eggs to bind everything, but if you plan on wrapping the stuffing with pastry, you can omit the eggs. Using puff pastry sheets makes this dessert ever so easy, convenient and quite decadent. It's an easy dessert for parties.

MAKES 2 (7", OR 18-CM) TARTS

⅓ cup (50 g) cashews

⅓ cup (50 g) raisins

1 tbsp (14 g) ghee or butter

½ cup (50 g) unsweetened dried coconut flakes

¾ cup (150 g) dried candied fruit (tutti-frutti or Christmas mixture of different colors)

¼ cup (50 g) sugar

⅓ tsp ground cardamom

2 eggs

2 sheets frozen puff pastry, defrosted

Egg wash (half an egg mixed with 1 tsp water) or whipping cream, for brushing the tops

Roughly chop the cashews and raisins. Melt the ghee in a nonstick pan over medium-low heat. Add the cashews and raisins and toast lightly, 1 minute. Add the coconut and cook for 2 minutes. Add the candied fruit and sugar and stir to combine. Turn off the heat and add the cardamom. Mix well and let cool. Once it is cool, add the eggs and mix well.

Preheat the oven to 400°F (200°C, or gas mark 6) for 15 minutes.

Line a nonstick round pan (which is traditionally used) or a square pan with the puff pastry and press up the sides. Trim the edges. Using a fork, pierce some holes in the bottom of the pastry so that it doesn't puff up too much. Brush with the egg wash and bake for 12 minutes. Remove the pan from the oven, pour the coconut mixture onto the puff pastry and bake for 15 minutes longer, or until the center is not wobbly and the coconut mixture is set.

HONEY CAKE

This is a very popular South Indian cake found in bakeries. It almost tastes the same and is an absolute favorite among friends, too. If you love honey and coconut, this might be something you will fall in love with. This sponge cake is doused with orange, honey and cardamom syrup, and it sits with the sweet syrup on top, slowly getting soaked in. The more it soaks, the better it gets.

MAKES 8" (20-CM) SQUARE CAKE

SYRUP

1½ cups (355 ml) water

1 cup (320 g) orange blossom honey

1 cup (100 g) coconut powder

¼ cup (60 ml) fresh squeezed orange juice

Drop of red food coloring (optional)

½ tsp freshly ground cardamom

CAKE

1 cup (225 g) butter

1 cup (200 g) sugar

4 large eggs

1 tsp vanilla extract

¼ cup (60 ml) milk

2 cups (240 g) all-purpose flour

1 tbsp (8 g) baking powder

Pinch of salt

Preheat the oven to 325°F (170°C, or gas mark 3). Grease an 8-inch (20-cm) cake pan.

To make the syrup, combine all the ingredients except for the cardamom in a pan over medium heat, bring to a boil and simmer it for 10 minutes. Remove from the heat, add the cardamom and let cool.

To make the cake, in a mixing bowl, whip the butter until it's light and fluffy. Add the sugar, ¼ cup (50 g) at a time, and beat well after each addition. Add the eggs, one at a time, along with vanilla and milk; beat well.

In a separate bowl, combine the flour, baking powder and salt. Fold it into the butter mixture, being careful not to overmix. Pour into the prepared cake pan and bake for 40 to 50 minutes, until a cake tester inserted into the middle comes out clean. Let the cake cool for 20 minutes.

Randomly pierce the cake with a wooden toothpick, give the syrup a good stir because the coconut tends to float and pour it over the cake. Let sit for at least 2 hours before serving.

ORANGE CHIFFON CAKE WITH PISTACHIO-CARDAMOM SWIRLS

By now you may have seen a pattern with my desserts. I like rustic, simple and non-fussy. This is one of the first cakes I developed many years ago and it has become a favorite. The orange and pistachio are a match made in heaven. This is a rich and moist cake that holds its shape very well if you want to make a layer cake.

MAKES ONE 8" (20-CM) CAKE

¼ cup (36 g) raw pistachios

1¼ cups (150 g) all-purpose flour

2 tbsp (16 g) cornstarch

1¼ cups (150 g) confectioners' sugar

2 tsp (6 g) baking powder

⅓ tsp ground cardamom

Pinch of salt

3 large eggs, separated, at room temperature

⅓ cup (80 ml) vegetable oil

½ cup (120 ml) orange juice

Zest of 1 orange

1 tsp vanilla extract

Slivered pistachios, for garnish

Lightly sweetened whipped cream, for serving (optional)

Soak the pistachios in water overnight. Drain, pat dry with paper towels and grind into a fine paste in a food processor; set aside.

Preheat the oven to 325°F (170°C, or gas mark 3). Grease an 8-inch (20-cm) pan.

Sift the flour, cornstarch, confectioners' sugar, baking powder, cardamom and salt into a large bowl. In a mixing bowl, whip the egg whites to soft peaks.

In a separate mixing bowl, beat the egg yolks, oil, orange juice, orange zest and vanilla. Add the dry ingredients and mix well to incorporate. Then fold in the egg whites in 3 additions to incorporate well. Scoop out ½ cup (120 ml) batter and fold in the pistachio paste.

Pour the plain batter into the prepared cake pan. Slowly pour the pistachio mixture in a circle and swirl it around carefully with a toothpick. Top with the slivered pistachios. Bake for 40 to 45 minutes, or until a toothpick inserted into the center comes out clean. Let cool for 20 minutes before slicing. Serve with whipped cream, if desired.

SESAME MINI CAKES WITH CHAI GLAZE

Sesame is an underestimated seed. It has a distinctively nutty flavor and is used a lot in Indian and Asian cooking. It has many good medicinal properties, too. Lightly toasted and powdered sesame seeds add a distinct flavor to dishes. In this I like how chai and sesame pair with each other. The cake itself is not too sweet, and the glaze really makes it come alive with the spices and sweet condensed milk.

MAKES 8-10 MINI CAKES

CAKE

2 cups (240 g) all-purpose flour

⅓ cup (40 g) black sesame powder

2 tsp (6 g) baking powder

½ tsp salt

½ tsp ground cardamom

¾ tsp ground ginger

⅛ tsp ground cloves

½ cup (112 g) unsalted butter, at room temperature

¾ cup (150 g) granulated sugar

2 large eggs, at room temperature

⅓ cup (80 ml) brewed black tea, at room temperature

½ cup (120 ml) whole milk, at room temperature

GLAZE

½ cup (120 ml) sweetened condensed milk

⅓ cup (40 g) confectioners' sugar

½ tsp ground cinnamon

2 tbsp (30 ml) brewed chai (tea), at room temperature

Preheat the oven to 350°F (180°C, or gas mark 4). Line 8 to 10 cups of a muffin tin with paper liners or butter and flour very well.

To make the cake, sift the flour, sesame powder, baking powder, salt, cardamom, ginger and cloves into a bowl and set aside.

In a stand mixer or using a whip or handheld mixer, beat the butter until creamy. Add the sugar and whip for 2 to 3 minutes longer, and then add the eggs and whip until the eggs are completely incorporated. Turn off the mixer, add the brewed tea, milk and sifted dry ingredients, and then turn on the mixer on low speed and beat only until everything is incorporated, about 10 seconds. Take the bowl out and with a spatula clean the sides and mix a couple of times so that there's no butter stuck to the bottom.

Use a large ice cream scoop to scoop the batter into the muffin tins. Bake for about 20 minutes, or until a toothpick inserted into the center of a cake comes out clean.

To make the glaze, in a small bowl, mix the condensed milk, confectioners' sugar, cinnamon and brewed chai until it is thick and a pourable consistency. Drizzle the glaze over the cooled cakes. Serve immediately or drizzle the glaze when you are ready to serve.

NO-CHURN COFFEE ICE CREAM WITH CASHEWS AND CHOCOLATE-CHILI DRIZZLE

It's no secret to my family and friends that I have an intense love-relationship with my coffee—filter coffee (a South Indian dark brewed coffee), to be exact. I don't make ice cream often. In retrospect, I don't really make it at all. When I do, it's this recipe using a method I learned from Nigella Lawson. As Nigella says, "It's almost embarrassing how simple this is." It's true!

MAKES 2 QUARTS (2 L)

1 quart (1 L) heavy whipping cream, chilled but not freezing

1 cup (235 ml) condensed milk

2 tsp (12 g) espresso or instant coffee powder, divided

¼ tsp ground cardamom

⅓ tsp vanilla extract

Chopped cashews, for serving

HARD SHELL

7 oz (196 g) bittersweet chocolate, chopped

2 tbsp (28 g) virgin coconut oil

Pinch of cayenne pepper

Wash and dry the mixing bowl very well. You can chill it a bit before using if you like.

In a stand mixer fitted with a whipping attachment, or using a handheld mixer, start whipping the cream on low speed until it has thickened and has a soft peak consistency. Add the condensed milk, 1 teaspoon of the espresso, cardamom and vanilla. Start whipping again and slowly increase the speed until you reach a stiff peak consistency, 3 to 5 minutes. Turn off the mixer. Add the remaining espresso and mix it in with a spatula, not completely, so you still see a swirl. Pour it in any freezer proof bowl. Top it with broken cashews. Cover and chill overnight.

To make the hard shell, melt the chocolate in a small metal bowl set over a pan of simmering water. Stir in the coconut oil and cayenne pepper and heat until dissolved, about 1 minute. Keep the liquid lukewarm until ready to serve. Chocolate will harden into a shell within a few seconds when spooned over ice cream.

Serve the ice cream with a drizzle of the chocolate.

FRUITY LASSI ICE POPS

Turn a drink into a frozen treat on a stick and it's so much better. Even better are the combination of different fruits in a traditional lassi. Fresh fruits are preferred, but if you have frozen, they work, too.

MAKES 4 ICE POPS

SIMPLE SYRUP

½ cup (120 ml) water

1 cup (200 g) sugar

MANGO LASSI

1 ripe yellow mango, peeled, seeded and diced

5 tbsp (75 ml) simple syrup, divided

⅓ tsp ground cardamom

1 cup (235 g) Greek yogurt

BLUEBERRY LASSI

1 cup (145 g) blueberries, stemmed

2 tbsp (25 g) sugar

½ cup (120 g) Greek yogurt

2 tbsp (30 ml) simple syrup

⅓ tsp ground ginger

STRAWBERRY LASSI

1 cup (145 g) ripe strawberries, stemmed

2 tbsp (25 g) sugar

½ cup (120 g) Greek yogurt

2 tbsp (30 ml) simple syrup

MINT-CUCUMBER LASSI

½ cup (40 g) packed mint leaves, washed well

½ cucumber, peeled and seeded

⅓ tsp chaat masala

½ cup (120 g) Greek yogurt

To make simple syrup, combine the water and sugar in a saucepan and bring to a simmer; simmer for 5 minutes. Remove from the heat and let it cool before using.

To make the mango lassi, in a blender, combine the mango, 2 tablespoons (30 ml) of the simple syrup and the cardamom and set aside. In a small bowl, mix the yogurt with the remaining simple syrup. Set both the mixtures in the refrigerator for about 1 hour. Then, add the mixture to 4 ice pop molds, alternating between the mango mixture and the yogurt mixture. Take a toothpick or skewer and swirl it lightly. Insert the top of the mold and place in the freezer for 4 to 5 hours, or until firm.

To make the blueberry lassi, combine the blueberries and sugar in a pot and simmer, mashing the blueberries with a wooden spoon, until the mixture turns a syrupy consistency, about 5 minutes. Transfer to a bowl, cover and refrigerate for 30 minutes. Combine the yogurt, simple syrup and ginger in a small bowl and refrigerate. Add a few tablespoons of the yogurt mixture to the ice pop molds, top with the blueberry mixture and swirl it with a clean skewer. Chill for 6 hours to overnight.

To make the strawberry lassi, combine the strawberries and sugar in a pot and simmer, mashing the berries with a wooden spoon, until the mixture turns a syrupy consistency, about 5 minutes. Transfer to a bowl, cover and refrigerate for 30 minutes. Combine the yogurt and simple syrup in a small bowl and refrigerate. Add a few tablespoons of the yogurt mixture to the ice pop molds, top with the strawberry mixture and swirl it with a clean skewer. Chill for 6 hours to overnight.

To make the mint-cucumber lassi, combine the mint, cucumber and chaat masala in a blender and blend. Gently mix in with the yogurt and chill for 30 minutes. Pour into molds and chill for 5 to 6 hours or overnight. To remove the pops from the molds, run under hot water until they are easily released.

CHAPTER 6

SAUCES, DIPS & CHUTNEYS

"Bottle that sauce," she says. I stare at her greenish blue eyes as she finishes the last drop of chutney in the bowl.

Rain slashed the trees, and the grass got greener as we stared at it. Winds blew with a blurry sound. It was a day to sit down for a good read and coffee. My friend called, and I jumped to invite her over for a chat. "Yes, I'll make my filter coffee and chutney with those fritters you like," I say even before she asks.

We've been at the table with pakoras and three different sauces for the last hour, chatting about why the school system needs to be reformed, what will happen if immigration laws were to be tightened, a must-read book, to "Oh, they broke up?" Today was a discussion, a talk on why women should empower other women.

"Why not? Why can't you bottle this sauce?" she continues.

"Sauces are like handmade pottery," I say. Each time, I make small quantities, and every single time, it's a tad bit different—maybe it's the consistency, a tad bit tangier or a bit more spicy.

To me, sauces are the key to making or breaking a dish. It has to be just perfectly paired, and it can transform a blah dish into a spectacular one. The Almond Curry Sauce (page 163), with a touch of mirin in it, just works so well in tacos, smeared first, not drizzled last. The last drizzle is the Apple Cilantro Chutney (page 162). When you take a bite, you first taste the bread, then the sweet curry and then the stuffing and then you finish off with the lemony, spicy green sauce. It's truly an experience. Each curry here works with many dishes, and all you need in your curry repertoire is right in this chapter.

Although bottling the sauce hasn't happened yet, my friend went home that day with four bottles, three different chutneys and a plum barbecue sauce.

APPLE CILANTRO CHUTNEY

As I always say, "Chutneys are like accessories; they are a must, but don't overdo it." I almost always have this chutney sitting in my refrigerator. What a pinch of salt does to a dessert, sugar—or in this, case apple—does to this is chutney. It's unexpected but works well. This is my basic green chutney that I use for chaat, tacos, burgers and fried food. I put it on everything: it's my go-to sauce, other than Sriracha.

MAKES 2 CUPS (240 G)

1 apple, cored and chopped

1 cup (32 g) packed cilantro, chopped

½ cup (48 g) packed mint leaves, chopped

2 tbsp (30 ml) lemon juice

1 tsp cumin seeds

¼ red onion, diced

2 cloves garlic

3 Thai green chiles

⅓ tsp salt

2 tsp (10 ml) vegetable oil

⅓ cup (80 ml) water

Place all the ingredients in a blender and grind to a paste. Transfer to an air-tight container and keep refrigerated for up to 3 to 4 days.

*See photo on page 160.

ALMOND CURRY SAUCE

Sweet, nutty and mildly hot from the Sriracha and curry powder, this sauce is the easiest way to create an impression. Play with the acidity and the nuts you prefer. Peanuts are great, and I've even used cashews. Or use a mix of nuts.

MAKES 1 CUP (235 ML)

⅓ cup (45 g) lightly toasted almonds

1 tbsp (8 g) sesame seeds

Juice from ½ lime

⅓ tsp red pepper flakes

1 tsp Sriracha or any hot sauce

1 tsp honey

4 cloves garlic, chopped

1 tsp mirin or sweet rice vinegar

¼ tsp curry powder

1 tsp olive oil

½ tsp cumin seeds

⅓ tsp roasted fennel seeds (optional)

1 scallion

3 tbsp (45 g) coconut cream

Place all of the ingredients in a food processor and grind to a smooth paste. Add a bit of hot water to thin, if needed. It should be of a pourable consistency. This can be stored in the refrigerator for up to 3 days.

*See photo on page 160.

Note: This can be a dressing for pasta, a dipping sauce or used for tacos.

YOGURT SAUCE

This sauce is ridiculously simple, but it brings a dish together while still keeping itself understated. Add diced cucumber, onion and tomatoes to make a raita. Add grated vegetables to make a vegetable dip. I love adding raw, grated beets to it. There are so many ways to amp it up.

MAKES 1 CUP (235 ML)

---

1 cup (235 g) thick full-fat yogurt (not the Greek kind)

Pinch of chili powder

⅓ tsp salt

¼ tsp sugar

⅓ tsp cumin seeds, toasted and coarsely crushed

Mix everything together and leave it in the refrigerator. Use it on sandwiches and with naan and curry.

*See photo on page 160.

HARISSA

Harissa is a spicy paste used as a staple in North African and Middle Eastern cooking, similar to Indian pickles. I love a little heat in my food. In fact, I need to almost feel the spice in every meal. So, Indian pickles and Sriracha are consumed in large quantities in our home. Harissa recipes vary between countries and regions, but coriander seeds and cumin are common in many. Spread it on sandwiches, smother it on chicken and spread it on tofu. I like it on everything!

MAKES 2 CUPS (300 G)

4 oz (112 g) dried chiles (I used Anaheim and New Mexico chiles)

2 oz (56 g) sun-dried tomatoes

1 tsp coriander seeds

1 tsp cumin seeds

1 tsp caraway seeds

3–4 cloves garlic

2 tbsp (30 g) tomato paste

1 tsp kosher salt, or to taste

⅓ cup (80 ml) vegetable oil

Place the chiles and sun-dried tomatoes in a heatproof bowl, cover with boiling water and soak for 30 minutes. Drain, reserving the soaking liquid, and set aside.

Dry-roast all the seeds and the garlic in a heavy-bottomed pan until you smell the spices, about 2 minutes. Transfer to a food processor or a blender, along with the softened chiles and sun-dried tomatoes and the tomato paste. Process to a smooth paste. If it is hard to process, add some of the soaking liquid a little at a time until you get a smooth mixture. Add the salt and process to combine. Transfer to an airtight glass container, cover with the vegetable oil and store for a month in the refrigerator. To use, mix the oil in well and use as desired.

MIXED FRUIT CARDAMOM JAM

My first experience of making jam was with my grandma. We made this mixed fruit jam every summer. She created some memories. I make jam every summer now. While it bubbles I go back in time, the warm embrace, the moments of laughter; it was a grounding experience. When I am teaching a class now, I always almost give the history of how a recipe was created and why it is important to me.

Jams are very easy to make. You can control the sugar and add a touch of your personality with the spice. It preserves well without the additives. This is the combo I usually make. If you haven't tried jam at home, you should; you will be addicted to making and sharing.

MAKES 2 QT (2 L)

4 Gala apples, unpeeled, cored and diced

2 cups (350 g) red grapes

3 bananas

2 cups (340 g) diced strawberries

2 plums, pitted and diced

Peel and juice of 1 large lemon

1 cup (200 g) sugar, or as needed

Pinch of salt

1 tsp cardamom

Place a metal spoon in the freezer. Wash and sterilize 4 pint-sized (470-ml) canning jars.

In a heavy-bottomed pan, preferably a steel or a copper pot, add all the cut fruits. Cut the lemon peel into large pieces so you can remove it later; add the peel to the pot along with the lemon juice, sugar and salt. Bring the mixture to a boil over medium-high heat, stirring constantly so the bottom doesn't scorch. Mash the fruits a bit with a masher. (Or you can use an electric blender later for a smoother texture.) Keep stirring for about 15 minutes. When you see the bubbles have become smaller, take out the spoon from the freezer, add a drop of the jam and see whether it sets. If it stays as a blob and doesn't spread, then your jam is done. Another way to test whether the jam is done is to place some on the spoon and then run your finger through it; if it leaves a path, then it's done. You can also place a small drop on a plate and see whether it spreads. Check for sweetness, and add more sugar as needed, stirring until combined. Jam is usually done in 20 to 25 minutes. Add the cardamom and stir to combine.

Ladle the jam into the sterilized jars. If you plan to use it throughout the year, boil the filled bottles in a huge pot filled with water for about 10 minutes. It will keep for up to a year if you properly can it and sterilize everything very well.

SPICY PLUM BARBECUE SAUCE

Make this when plums are in season, bottle it and refrigerate. Toss it with pasta or use it as a sauce with your favorite meat. This recipe was a happy accident. One summer when I attempting to make plum jam, halfway through I realized the plums were not sweet at all. In fact, they were tart like crazy. I added some spices, tinkered with it a bit and now this is one of my favorite sauces. My friend Abi is a spokesperson for how delicious this sauce is!

MAKES 1 QUART (1 L)

3 lb (1.3 kg) red plums, pitted and chopped

½ cup (112 g) packed brown sugar

6 cloves garlic, lightly crushed with the back of a knife

1 tbsp (5 g) coriander seeds

3 thin slices lemon

1 tsp cumin seeds

1 tsp red pepper flakes or black peppercorns

4 sage leaves

¼ cup (60 ml) apple cider vinegar

1 tbsp (9 g) garlic powder

1" (2.5-cm) piece ginger, peeled and finely grated

1 tbsp (9 g) red chili powder

2 tsp (12 g) salt

¼ tsp Worcestershire sauce

Add the pitted plums and brown sugar to a large, heavy-bottomed deep pan. Place the crushed garlic, coriander, lemon slices, cumin, red pepper flakes and sage in the center of a piece of cheesecloth. Pull the corners into a bundle and tie it tightly. Add the packet to the plum mixture along with the apple cider vinegar, garlic powder, ginger, red chili powder, salt and Worcestershire sauce and bring the mixture to a boil over medium heat, stirring continuously. Decrease to a simmer and cook for 40 to 45 minutes. Remove from the heat and let cool.

Once the sauce is a bit cooled, remove the cheesecloth and press on it hard with the back of a wooden spoon to extract as much flavor as possible. Transfer to a large strainer set over a bowl and strain the sauce so that you get a good consistency without any pulp. Return the strained sauce to the same pan and bring it to a simmer over medium-low heat. Check for spices, and add anything you want accordingly. Simmer for 15 more minutes, then remove from the heat and let cool.

Pour the sauce into 2 pint-sized (470-ml) jars and store refrigerated for up to a month or at room temperature for a week.

ONION TOMATO CHUTNEY

You can use any variety of tomato for this satisfying chutney. Put it on sandwiches, have it as a dip or mix it with some olive oil and make it into a dressing. I love it with dosas or any flatbread. The variety of ways that you can use this chutney is endless. Try adding a few carrots or another vegetable while you cook the onions; this recipe is just a template. Make it your own!

MAKES 1 CUP (255 G)

2 tbsp (30 ml) vegetable oil

6–8 dried red chiles

2 tbsp (20 g) split black gram

1 red onion, chopped

1 tsp salt, divided

3 tomatoes, cored and quartered

1" (2.5-cm) piece dried tamarind or ⅓ tsp tamarind concentrate

2" (5-cm) piece jaggery or panela, crushed, or 2 tbsp (30 g) brown sugar

Heat the oil in a pan over medium heat. Let it get hot and then add the red chiles and split black gram. Let them pop and sauté a bit, but do not let the chiles become too brown. Add the onion and a pinch of the salt and continue to sauté until the onions are golden brown, about 2 minutes. Add the tomatoes and remaining 1 teaspoon salt and sauté, stirring, for about 3 minutes, or until it all comes together and the tomatoes have disintegrated. Remove from the heat. Add the tamarind and jaggery and stir to combine. Let the chutney cool completely, and then transfer to a food processor and process into a fine paste.

*See photo on page 160.

COCONUT CHUTNEY

This chutney is quintessential to South Indian homes. Everyone has their tips and tricks to make it their own and special. I learned this recipe from my aunt, who makes it so well that I had to find out her trade secret.

MAKES 1 CUP (120 G)

1 tsp chana dal or split Bengal gram dal

½ tsp cumin seeds

1 tsp vegetable oil, divided

½ cup (40 g) packed freshly grated or frozen coconut

1″ (2.5-cm) piece fresh tamarind

⅓ tsp salt

4 green chiles, seeded for less heat if desired

4 leaves coriander (from 1 stem)

⅓ cup (80 ml) water

¼ tsp black mustard seeds

Pinch of asafetida

10 leaves fresh curry (optional)

In a skillet over medium heat, toast the chana dal and cumin seeds with ¼ teaspoon of the oil until brown and toasted, 1 minute.

In a blender, combine the coconut, chana-cumin mixture, tamarind, salt, chiles, coriander leaves and water and grind to a coarse paste.

In a small sauté pan over medium heat, add the remaining ¾ teaspoon oil and let it get hot. Add the mustard seeds, asafetida and curry leaves, if using, and let them pop and then immediately add to the chutney. This chutney is best used immediately or within the next day or two; keep it refrigerated if you plan on using it the next day.

CHAPTER 7

DRINKS

As Humphrey Bogart said, "The problem with the world is that everyone is a few drinks behind." Come to think of it, drinks are like the main characters in a movie. They appear in the beginning, stay throughout and are there for the finale.

I love mixology, both virgin and not, but I don't like it when drinks get so complex that they become impractical. Drinks make everyone feel special. I've always loved pouring them into fun glasses. I have many friends who don't drink alcohol, and some who do, so I almost always have two options of the same drink.

I love the unexpected twist of poppy seeds in a drink, as in the Khus Khus Coconut Milk Cooler (page 173). The Carrot Halwa and Watermelon Colada (page 175) is like a dessert and drink in one. Ginger has to be one of my favorite things to add to cocktails for its fresh and spicy touch. Add it to a margarita (page 174) and taste the subtle difference. Lychees are another one of my favorite fruits to add to cocktails, and the Lychee Mint Lemonade (page 172) is just going to blow you away.

A great story begins with a drink in the hand, so cheers. Make it happen.

LYCHEE MINT LEMONADE

This is a refreshing and unexpected twist to lemonade. Lychee has a floral hint to it and mellows the lemon. Canned lychees are great if you can't find fresh ones.

SERVES 6

30 lychees, peeled and pitted, or 1 (15-oz [420-g]) can lychees in syrup

Juice of 2 limes

Juice of 4 lemons

4 cups (940 ml) water

¼ cup (50 g) sugar

2 sprigs mint

Ice

Crush the lychees in a pitcher with a muddler. Add everything else except the ice and stir until all the sugar dissolves. Serve chilled over ice.

*See photo on page 170.

KHUS KHUS COCONUT MILK COOLER

Poppy seeds have an aromatic, nutty flavor and are used commonly in India. Soaking the poppy seeds in hot water helps when you are ready to grind them. I enjoy this drink on a cool summer day, or serve it warm with a scoop of your favorite ice cream as a dessert.

SERVES 2

2 tbsp (12 g) white poppy seeds (khus khus), soaked in hot water for 30 minutes

3 whole cardamom pods

1 cup (80 g) freshly grated coconut or 2 cups (470 ml) light coconut milk

2 cups (355 ml) hot water (if using fresh coconut), divided

2 tbsp (25 g) sugar

Pinch of ground ginger

Lots of ice

In a blender, grind the poppy seeds, cardamom, fresh coconut and ½ cup (120 ml) of the water to a smooth puree. Using a piece of cheesecloth or a fine strainer, strain the coconut milk puree, so you don't get the coarse coconut and bits of poppy seeds in your drink. Add the remaining 1½ cups (355 ml) water to the mixture, along with the sugar and ginger. Mix very well, chill and serve over ice.

*See photo on page 170.

Note: If you are using coconut milk, omit the water. Just grind the poppy seeds with ½ cup (120 ml) of the coconut milk and cardamom, strain and then add the remaining 1½ cups (355 ml) coconut milk.

PINEAPPLE GINGER MARGARITA

My love for some heat doesn't stop with food—it goes for cocktails, too. You are in for a treat when the heat from this margarita hits your throat along with the warmth of the tequila. Reduce the amount of the jalapeño if you want to cut down the heat. This pairs well with tacos, grilled chicken or Pita Wraps (page 85).

SERVES 1

4 chunks fresh pineapple

4 thin slices jalapeño

1" (2.5-cm) piece ginger, peeled and thinly sliced

4 tsp (20 ml) tequila

4 tsp (20 ml) triple sec

4 tsp (20 ml) pineapple juice

1 tbsp (15 ml) lime juice

Ice

Salt and pepper, for the rim

Jalapeño and pineapple skewer, for garnish

In a cocktail shaker, add the pineapple chunks, jalapeño and ginger. Using a muddler or the back of a wooden ladle, crush the ingredients lightly. Add the tequila, triple sec, pineapple juice and lime juice and stir. Add ice and shake until the shaker is completely chilled. Pour into a margarita glass rimmed with salt and pepper. Add the skewer garnish and serve immediately.

*See photo on page 170.

CARROT HALWA AND WATERMELON COLADA

I always say that desserts are great on their own, but mix in some alcohol and they are epic. This colada is a must-try, with or without alcohol. The sweet juicy watermelon, coconut flavors and carrot juice give this drink a strong character. Make sure you use ripe sweet watermelon and coconut cream, not coconut milk.

SERVES 2

2 carrots, washed, peeled and finely grated

½ cup (120 ml) whole milk

3 tbsp (36 g) sugar

⅓ tsp ground cardamom

1 cup (150 g) fresh or frozen watermelon chunks

1 oz (30 ml) white rum

4 oz (120 ml) coconut rum

⅓ cup (80 ml) coconut cream; if using canned, discard the water and use the top cream.

Ice

In a saucepan, combine the grated carrots, milk and sugar. Bring it to a boil and then simmer for 5 minutes. The mixture should be thick and the carrots should be cooked by now. Turn off the heat and add the ground cardamom. Let it cool completely. This is the carrot halwa.

In a blender, combine the watermelon, white rum, coconut rum, coconut cream and carrot halwa and blend very well to a smooth consistency. Pour into glasses with a little ice and serve.

*See photo on page 170.

Note: You can make the carrot halva earlier so you have it when you are ready to make the drink.

You can leave the rum out completely to make it a nonalcoholic drink.

CHAPTER 8

SPICES & INGREDIENTS

Spices, herbs and seasonings are the first thing you taste when you take a bite of food, so not overusing them, keeping them fresh and adding them at the right time of cooking is key.

SPICES

I have tried to use a minimum of spices. Here, I've listed the ingredients that will help you make any dish from this book. The key thing to remember is to store these spices in glass jars in a cool place. You can find all of these ingredients in an Indian grocery store or online.

AMCHOOR (DRY MANGO POWDER)

This is strong, tart powder made from green mangoes. It has quite a unique flavor and adds a lemony touch to dishes where it's called for. This is used a lot in North Indian cooking and chaat. I like adding mango powder on freshly cut pineapple or in a glass of orange juice. You can find this in boxed form at any Asian grocery store.

ASAFETIDA

This very popular spice used in Indian cooking is also known as hing or perungayam. It belongs to the fennel and onion family and is quite pungent—a little goes a long way! It's almost always fried in oil to remove the bitterness. There are two forms of asafetida. One is the solid form, which is stronger in flavor. You have to break or powder this to use it in curries and dishes. The other, more popular form is the powder you get in a white plastic bottle. This stays fresh for a year. Asafetida is used mostly in tempering the oil before the onion or tomato goes into a dish.

BAY LEAF

This fragrant leaf from the laurel tree surprisingly gets stronger as it dries. Fresh bay leaves are shiny green on top and dull and lighter underneath. Bay leaves are essential for rich vegetarian curries and meat dishes. They are not edible, so discard them after the dish is cooked. You can store them in a zip-top bag and they will stay good for years.

BLACK MUSTARD SEEDS

Although there are many different kinds of mustard seeds, I have used black mustard seeds throughout this book for many dishes. I don't know a South Indian dish, other than meat preparations, that doesn't use mustard seeds. The potent brown and black seeds are popular in Indian cuisine and especially in curries, where they lend a more subtle heat than chiles or peppercorns. The seeds pop when you add them to hot oil and that's when you know they've flavored the oil and it's ready for the other ingredients. Using this raw, ground up in dishes is very popular in parts of India.

BLACK ONION/NIGELLA SEEDS

These seeds, which are rougher in shape than sesame seeds, are also called kalonji in India. They have a mild and nutty, oniony flavor and go perfectly with Middle Eastern flatbreads and the Mangalore buns (page 33) in this book. Black onion seeds work beautifully in some vegetarian curries. Use them toasted and sprinkled on potatoes for an extra crunch and flavor.

BLACK PEPPERCORNS

Coming from the berries of a pepper plant, black peppercorn is one of the most used spices in South Indian cooking. The kernels are dried in the sun or by machine for several days, during which the pepper around the seed shrinks and darkens into a thin, wrinkled layer. Using freshly ground pepper is always recommended. Add a touch of pepper to finish a curry and it elevates the flavors. No wonder they call it the "king of spices" and it is the world's most traded spice.

CARAWAY SEEDS

Caraway seeds look very similar to cumin. In fact, they are cousins, but cumin is sweet and caraway is pungent, so you have to use it sparingly. The seeds are highly aromatic and very distinctive in flavor. They can be boiled in water and kept in clay pots, then used to ease digestion, which is what they used to do in summers in India.

CHAAT MASALA

This is a mix of pepper, mango powder, black salt and a few other spices. Get a box of this and you can use it on your favorite fruits, in drinks and in the popular chaat. You can find great quality chaat powder in stores and online. It's easy to transform a dish with just a pinch of chaat masala.

CHILI POWDER

There are many different varieties of chili powder. When an Indian recipe calls for chili powder, it is usually pure red hot chiles ground into a fine powder. Indian chili powder is not exactly the same thing as cayenne pepper, but you can freely substitute one for the other—the former you can find at any Indian grocer. Generally, some of the chili powders you get here might have some cumin or something else added in it. This book calls for plain chili powder. It is hot, so use accordingly. There's also another variety of chili powder I use called Kashmiri red chili powder (see page 179).

CINNAMON

Possibly the most common baking spice, cinnamon is used in cakes, cookies and desserts throughout the world. Cinnamon is also used in savory chicken and lamb dishes throughout India and the Middle East, where it is appreciated for its earthy and woodsy flavor. In American cooking, cinnamon is often paired with apples and used in other fruit and cereal dishes. Cinnamon sticks are used in pickling and for flavoring hot beverages.

CLOVES

Cloves are pretty little dried spices that are like unopened flower buds on a tree. Another spice best used sparingly, cloves can be powdered or left whole. Whole cloves can be discarded before serving or left in for the spice to soak into the dish and add more flavor. You can store them for years in airtight containers.

COCONUT

Many parts of India use a lot of coconut in every form—freshly grated coconut, coconut oil, dried coconut and coconut milk. Because it's sometimes hard to come by fresh coconut in the United States, and when you do it's a chore to break them open and grate the meat, you can use frozen, unsweetened grated coconut. Many Indian stores carry frozen grated coconut. If you don't have access to an Indian grocer or can't find frozen coconut, desiccated coconut can be used. Just rehydrate the dried coconut by soaking it in boiling water for 15 minutes.

COCONUT MILK

Curries almost always use some coconut milk. I am a big believer in using canned coconut milk, just for the ease of it. Making fresh coconut milk, though, is simple and delicious. When a recipe calls for thin coconut milk, just scoop away the cream and use only the watery part. For regular coconut milk, shake the can well and use the blended liquid.

CORIANDER SEEDS

These are small brown seeds that are dried. They are used ground up and whole for pickling. Lightly toast them to get the most flavor out of them. The seed has a flavor I would describe as bright, floral and slightly lemony, but is overall mild. The herb tastes more piney, green with citrus peel notes and is overall more pungent. This book calls for coriander seeds and cilantro/coriander leaves, which are totally different.

CUMIN SEEDS

Known as jeera in India, cumin is another spice that is commonly used in everyday Indian cooking. They come from the parsley family and resemble caraway seeds. While caraway is pungent and strong, cumin seeds are subtle and quite uniquely sweet. They can be ground up and added to dishes; when the seeds are dry roasted and powdered, it adds a special savory touch to fruits. The seeds can also be frozen to prolong their shelf life.

FENNEL SEEDS

Fennel seeds are a warm, aromatic spice used in sweet and savory dishes. I've seen people use them in chai, and desserts with fennel are absolutely divine. It is greener than cumin and more pungent. Fennel seeds, along with cumin seeds, are coated with sugar and spices such as jaggery and mango powder and served as a digestive aid in India. You see bowlfuls of this offered in almost all Indian restaurants.

FENUGREEK

Fenugreek, also known as meethi, is a unique-tasting brown seed that is widely used in Indian cuisine and for other purposes. All the parts of the fenugreek plant are used in cooking. The fresh green leaves are used in flatbreads and dry potato curries, and the dried leaves are sprinkled on curries to add that extra oomph. The seeds, lightly toasted and powdered, work great in chicken curries. The seeds have medicinal properties and are said to aid insomnia and gastrointestinal distress.

GREEN CARDAMOM

This is probably my second most favorite spice and I've used a lot of it in this book. There are two kinds of cardamom, the black larger one and the green one. I have used only the green one in this book. It is a green pod that has tiny precious, black beadlike seeds inside. Toasting it lightly in a dry pan will bring out more flavor. You can also grind it up along with the green outer pod. This is probably one of those spices that you want to buy whole and grind it when you need to.

JAGGERY

Jaggery is also known as vellam or gud. It is the unrefined, non-distilled sugar made from sugarcane. We use it in desserts and it balances the spice and works wonders in tamarind-based curries. There are few varieties of jaggery: the light kind and the dark kind. You can find them in blocks or circles. I like to buy the dark variety, which is smokier. When ready to make something out of this, you can shave them or break them. Some varieties have a bit of dirt in them, so boiling it first in water is advised. Break or crush a block of jaggery and add it to ½ cup (120 ml) water. Boil the mixture until the dirt falls to the bottom of the pot, then gently pour off the liquid and strain through a piece of cheesecloth.

KASHMIRI RED CHILI POWDER

Also known as deggi mirch, this powder is made from Kashmiri chiles, which are small and less spicy than other chiles, but lend an incomparable, vibrant red color and smoky flavor to dishes. If you can't come by Kashmiri red chili powder, often sold in Asian grocery stores, you can use paprika.

ROSE WATER

Rose water is simply water that is infused with real rose petals. It is so good in desserts. Add it at the end, so the aroma doesn't evaporate. You can find it in Indian grocery stores and online. Keep refrigerated.

SAFFRON

Saffron is made from the stigmas of a small purple crocus (*Crocus sativa*). Each flower contains only three of the yellow-orange stigmas, which must be handpicked, making saffron the world's most expensive spice. Thankfully, a little saffron goes a long way. It has a pungent, aromatic and earthy flavor and gives everything cooked with it a brilliant yellow tint. I have used saffron in many dishes in this book. Use a few strands, crushed with your fingers and soaked in a tablespoon (15 ml) of milk for optimal release of its flavor and color.

TAMARIND

India is now the world's largest producer of tamarind, which grows on a tree. Inside the podlike fruit, which is also called a legume, is a sticky pulp with seeds. Sweet but tart, and sometimes very sour, tamarind is potent. A little goes a long way. It comes in a concentrated paste form and in blocks. I prefer the block form; just soak it in warm water, drain it, discard the seeds and use the resulting paste. If you cannot get the blocks, try getting a milder, lighter colored concentrate. You might have to water it down before using it in recipes. Do not use the concentrate directly. Although tamarind pulp can be eaten alone, it is most often mixed with sugar or diluted to mellow the strong flavor. Tamarind is also the secret ingredient in Worcestershire sauce and is a great meat tenderizer.

TURMERIC

This beautiful yellow spice has been used in Indian cooking for thousands of years and it has a wide range of health benefits. It's considered an anti-inflammatory and antioxidant. This is one of those spices found in the spice *dabba* (box) in every Indian kitchen. It adds color, but too much of it can overwhelm a dish. If you can find fresh turmeric, it is great in pickles and smoothies. However, the dried powder is most commonly used. It does stain your fingers, so be careful.

OTHER INDIAN INGREDIENTS

A number of other ingredients are important in the Indian kitchen.

ALL-PURPOSE FLOUR

This is also called maida in India and is an essential ingredient for every baker. I always get unbleached all-purpose flour, which works in all kinds of baking and flatbreads.

DALS

Dals are also known as pulses, and there are several kinds, including the popular toor or tuvar dal, the split dal and the whole mung (green) dal. There are also lentils, which hold their shape and are great in staple dishes.

GHEE

Ghee creates magic when used in food, but use it sparingly. Ghee is made by melting butter over medium-low heat until simmering. As the water in the butter slowly evaporates, the milk solids sink to the bottom of the pan. After all the water has evaporated (the butter will stop making a sputtering sound), it is removed from the heat and poured through a cheesecloth-lined strainer to remove the milk solids. You're left with pure butterfat (aka clarified butter), though it is cooked a bit longer. At first it is a dark amber color. Bottle it up, and as it cools, it will turn pale yellow and solidify. Store it at room temperature to maintain the coarse texture of the ghee.

GRAM FLOUR

Also known as besan or chickpea flour, gram flour is widely used in India, mainly to make fritters and the popular yogurt-based curries. It is a soft yellow, fine powder that can also be used as a thickener.

RICE

The rice that I've used in this book is sona masoori. Lighter, medium-sized and very tasty, it is not as perfumed as basmati rice, so it's used a lot in everyday Indian cooking. Soaking the rice for 20 to 30 minutes before cooking it will give you the fluffiest grains. You can find this in any Indian grocery store. If you can't find it, you can use Blue Ribbon long-grain rice instead.

RICE FLOUR

This fine flour is milled from rice grains. It gives fritter batters a slight crunch, and pancakes made from rice flour are delicious and gluten free. It's a great alternative to wheat and all-purpose flour.

SEMOLINA

Semolina is a coarse yellow flour made from durum wheat. It gives a nutty, sweet flavor and mild yellow color to pasta, pizza and crêpes. You can substitute it for all-purpose flour for the added texture and nutrition or use it instead of cornmeal. It is so tasty in porridges and widely used in southern India.

VEGETABLE OIL

This is one of the most popular oils used in Indian cooking for deep-frying and for curries. It is flavorless and doesn't add or take away from the taste of a dish. The high smoke point of vegetable oil makes it a must when deep-frying.

WHOLE WHEAT FLOUR

This is more wholesome and browner and it is plain ground up wheat berries, which is sifted to get the smooth flour. I prefer whole wheat flour that has a bit of wheat germ in it. It makes for a hearty and healthier flatbread.

TIPS AND TRICKS

- While making a curry, always fry the onion, ginger, garlic and spices in oil over low heat until you see the oil ooze. That way you don't get the raw flavor of the spices and you don't burn them.

- Soak rice for 30 minutes, add a touch of lemon juice to the water and cook for softer, separated grains.

- Do not add salt while cooking lentils, because they will toughen up. Add a pinch of asafetida and turmeric.

- Oil your hands while you prepare onions, garlic and turmeric. You will avoid staining your fingers and your hands won't smell.

- Peel garlic and put it in an airtight container or zip-top bag and then freeze. This will make meal prep a bit easier.

- Peel and thinly slice ginger and freeze in a zip-top bag; it will stay fresh longer.

- Make a paste of ginger and garlic and freeze it in ice cube trays. Once frozen, pop them out, put them in bags and leave in the freezer. When you are ready to use, just add it directly to your cooking. Grind them with a little bit of oil and salt to extend their shelf life.

- When chopping vegetables for a stir-fry, chop extra and put them in bags for later use.

- Add a touch of salt when you want to sweat onions; that way, you don't need as much oil. Add a touch of sugar when you want to crisp and brown onions.

- Season with salt every step of the way to build your flavors.

- Add some olive oil to green chutneys to retain their color: it will look glossy and fresh.

ACKNOWLEDGMENTS

"One day, I will write a book," I used to say. And that dream came true. What a joy it was to create this baby. It took a team, and I am ever so grateful for that. It brought out the most vulnerable side of me, with so many emotions. Still, I would do it all over again. I come from a big fat Indian family and I am a crazy emotional person. So my list is long.

There is no way this book would have come to be without my readers, and I am so grateful for your constant support. A huge shout-out to the readers of my blog, supporters of my food and the friends I've made along the way. I truly believe my dream has come true because of you.

My beautiful boys, Nikhil and Adil. I truly feel honored to be your mom. You both were so supportive, so understanding and empathetic. You still wanted to be my hand models after so many arguments on how your fingers should be placed. My heart swells just saying your names. Every single shoot day for the book was fun for you, with all that food. But you always came home wanting to see the pictures first. God is great. I live for you. And everything I am is because of you and everything I do is for you.

My husband, my honey. You taught me to hold a camera, you gifted me the best ones. You introduced me to photography. You were the first one to admire my food. You tolerated my impatience at learning. You let me be me. You let me follow my heart and choose my path. Thank you, for everything.

My parents. Mom and Daddy, your love is unparalleled and unconditional. Dad, your discipline and the ability to carry on a routine are beyond amazing. You taught me to eat with your eyes first, and that stuck.

My friends, who've been a huge support system. If it weren't for you, asking for recipes, appreciating my food, I wouldn't be here.

My aunts, uncles and cousins. Your love and support mean the world to me.

Abi, what would I do without your humor and support? You were the one, the first person to ask me, "When are you writing a book, girl?" Here it is, with my heart poured in.

Deborah, my mentor, my strength. The quick question, turned into an hour-long conversation. You believed in me and held my hand throughout. I don't even want to think what I would do without you.

My best friend, Lakshmi. There's a quote: "In life, we never lose friends, we only know who the true ones are." You are one of the few. The blog brought us back together after years. You supported me throughout the process, helped with editing, listened to me whine and soothed me when I cried like a baby. You probably have no clue how much your presence means to me.

Alanna, you gave life to my recipes. You breathed a breath of beautiful fresh air into these pictures. Your support has been immense, and I am deeply grateful.

My dear friends Sangita, Shekhar, Bansi, Bina, Katyayini, Shilpa, Amisha, Priya, Swapna, Kani and Suja. You believed in me, cheered me on and most of all stuck with me throughout.

My food sisters, for all the love you've shown in the past year. Abi, Deborah, Naomi, Jen, Hazel and Susy, thank you.

All my lovely recipe testers from different continents. I am so thankful for all your time, effort and feedback. Your enthusiasm and willingness to support me are immeasurable.

Marissa and the team at Page Street. You have been patient and so very supportive. Thanks for giving me the opportunity to share what I had to offer.

And special thanks to Nik. Who would've thought that evening when we sat building my blog that it would turn into this? Thanks for editing all my posts and for all your creative ideas. I especially appreciate your knowledge of words and reading, your empathic and caring nature, your nonjudgmental attitude, and your honesty and ability to talk sense into me at times when I needed it. You make me want to be a better person every day.

Sesame–Peanuts
Brittle with
Rose Water

ABOUT THE AUTHOR

Asha Shivakumar is a writer, a storyteller and a self-taught cook. She believes life is more beautiful with food. Her blog, Food Fashion Party, focuses on real, everyday food with a twist. Her approachable personality and style of food convey to her readers that cooking doesn't have to be a chore. Shivakumar was named one of the top 10 Indian bloggers by the Huffington Post. She writes for magazines and her work is featured in *Food & Wine*. Nigella Lawson featured her as a follow-of-the-day on Instagram. Sharing food and stories has been her dream and she is living it.

INDEX